Vegetarian

2 Books In 1: 77 Recipes (x2) To Prepare Vegetarian Mexican Food At Home

By

Adele Tyler

Mexican Tacos Cookbook

77 Recipes for Preparing Traditional Mexican Tacos at Home with Fresh and Spicy Ingredients

By

Adele Tyler

© **Copyright 2020 by Adele Tyler - All rights reserved.**

This document is geared towards providing exact and reliable information in regard to the topic and issue covered. The publication is sold with the idea that the publisher is not required to render accounting, officially permitted, or otherwise, qualified services. If advice is necessary, legal or professional, a practiced individual in the profession should be ordered.

From a Declaration of Principles which was accepted and approved equally by a Committee of the American Bar Association and a Committee of Publishers and Associations.

In no way is it legal to reproduce, duplicate, or transmit any part of this document in either electronic means or in printed format. Recording of this publication is strictly prohibited and any storage of this document is not allowed unless with written permission from the publisher. All rights reserved.

The information provided herein is stated to be truthful and consistent, in that any liability, in terms of inattention or otherwise, by any usage or abuse of any policies, processes, or directions contained within is the solitary and utter responsibility of the recipient reader. Under no circumstances will any legal responsibility or blame be held against the publisher for any reparation, damages, or monetary loss due to the information herein, either directly or indirectly.

Respective authors own all copyrights not held by the publisher.

The information herein is offered for informational purposes solely and is universal as so. The presentation of the information is without contract or any type of guarantee assurance.

The trademarks that are used are without any consent, and the publication of the trademark is without permission or backing by the trademark owner.

All trademarks and brands within this book are for clarifying purposes only and are owned by the owners themselves, not affiliated with this document.

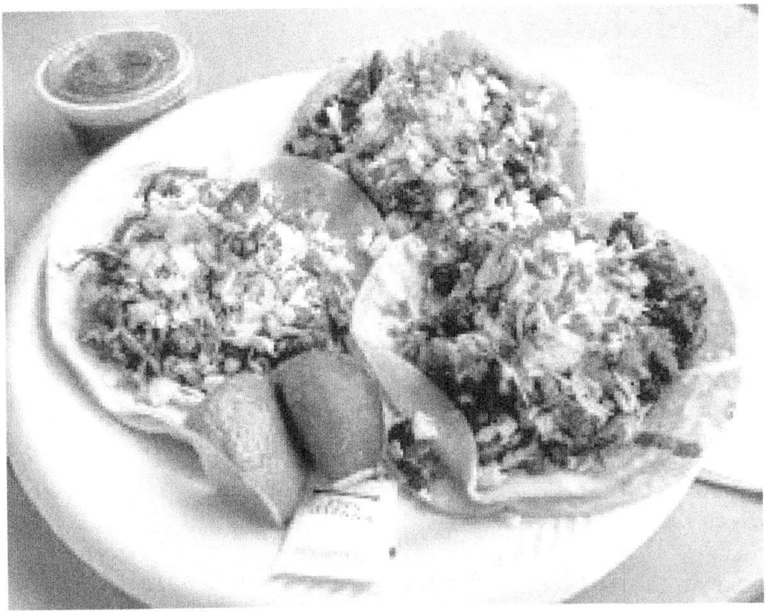

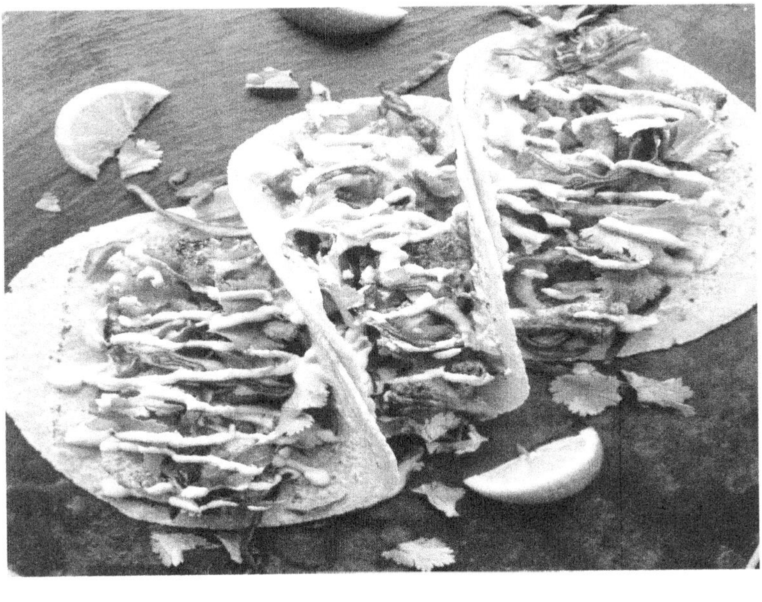

Table of contents

INTRODUCTION 11

CHAPTER 1: WELCOME TO THE WORLD OF MEXICAN TACO BREAKFAST RECIPES 13

1.1 Authentic Mexican Breakfast Taco 13

1.2 Tex-Mex Breakfast Taco 14

1.3 Chorizo and Egg Breakfast Taco 15

1.4 Migas Breakfast Taco 16

1.5 Mexican Street Taco 17

1.6 Mexican Taco Breakfast Burrito 18

1.7 Quick Breakfast Taco 19

1.8 Scrambled Egg Taco 20

1.9 Breakfast Taco with Avocado Cream 20

1.10 Chorizo and Potato Breakfast Taco 21

1.11 Pancake Breakfast Taco 22

1.12 Paleo Breakfast Taco 23

CHAPTER 2: MEXICAN TACO LUNCH RECIPES 25

2.1 Smoky Pork and Black Bean Taco 25

2.2 Grilled Salmon Tacos 26

2.3 Chipotle Chicken Tacos 27

2.4 Meatball Tacos 28

2.5 Prawn Tacos 29

2.6 Mexican Pulled Pork Tacos 29

2.7 Speedy Beef Tacos 30

2.8 Chipotle Cod Tacos 31

2.9 Tex-Mex Beef Tacos 32

2.10 Turkey Chili and Rice Tacos 33

2.11 Fish Finger Tacos 34

2.12 Fish Tacos with Chili Cream and Jalapeño Salsa 34

2.13 Crispy Chicken and Pineapple Tacos 35

2.14 Crab and Avocado Tacos 36

2.15 BBQ Bean Tacos 37

CHAPTER 3: MEXICAN TACO DINNER RECIPES 38

3.1 Kingfish Ceviche Tacos 38

3.2 Taco Rice with Grilled Chicken and Green Chili Salsa 39

3.3 Chicken Tacos with Charred Corn 40

3.4 Tacos de Carne Asada 41

3.5 Kingfish Ceviche Tacos with Tabasco 42

3.6 Quick Chicken Tacos with Homemade Hot Sauce 42

3.7 Slow Cooker Green Chili Chicken Tacos 43

3.8 Chicken and Avocado Taco with Creamy Cilantro Sauce ...44

3.9 Blackened Salmon Tacos 45

3.10 Spicy Shrimp Tacos with Creamy Sirarcha Sauce and Cilantro Lime Slaw..46

3.11 Roasted Cauliflower Tacos...46

3.12 Spicy Chicken and Kidney Bean Tacos...47

3.13 Pork Tacos with Dill and Apple Coleslaw 48

3.14 Taco Pull Apart...49

3.15 Cheesy Shell Tacos...50

CHAPTER 4: MEXICAN TACO SNACK RECIPES...............52

4.1 Corn and Cottage Cheese Tacos...52

4.2 Mini Chicken Taco Cups..53

4.3 Taco Bites..54

4.4 Mini Beef and Cheese Tacos 55

4.5 Taco Pinwheels...56

4.6 Mini Shrimp Tacos 57

4.7 Taco Wanton Cups 58

4.8 Turkey Taco Cups 59

4.9 Shrimp Taco Bites 60

4.10 Taco Cupcakes..61

4.11 Tacos Dorados 62

4.12 Taco Fries 63

4.13 Chicharrons Tacos..64

4.14 Rolled Taco Dip 65

4.15 Tangy Taco Tarts 66

CHAPTER 5: MEXICAN TACO VEGETARIAN RECIPES .67

5.1 Vegan Street Tacos 67

5.2 Quinoa Taco Meat 68

5.3 Black Beans and Zucchini Tacos 69

5.4 Lentil Tacos 71

5.5 Black Bean Tacos 72

5.6 Kidney Bean Fajita Tacos 73

5.7 Cauliflower Walnut Taco 74

5.8 Tofu Tacos 75

5.9 Quorn Chili Taco 76

5.10 Vegan Birria Tacos 77

5.11 Tacos Al Pastor 78

5.12 Tex- Mex Vegetarian Tacos 79

5.13 Jackfruit Tacos 80

5.14 Zucchini and Crimini Tacos 81

5.15 Potato Tacos 82

5.16 Vegetarian Taco Lasagna 83

5.17 Mushroom Tacos 84

5.18 Chickpea and Cauliflower Tacos 85

5.19 Pumpkin Tacos 86

5.20 Mexican Zucchini Tacos 87

CONCLUSION 89

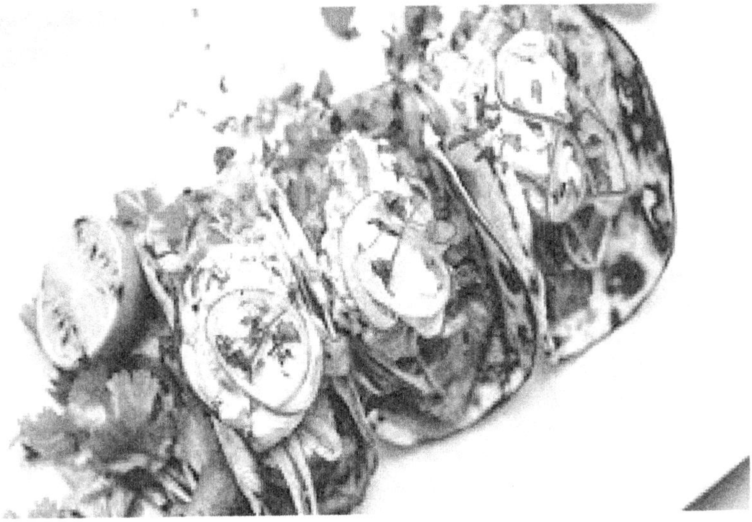

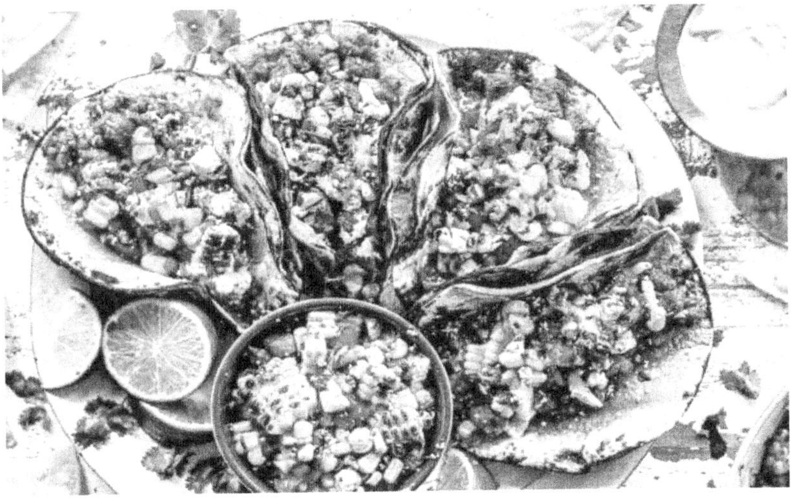

Introduction

One of the world's incredible cooking styles, Mexican food is delicious, as well as diverse and significantly omnivorous. The Mexican cooking style is both sophisticated and also simple. Food is of great value to Mexican culture, and eating admirably is something appreciated all through Mexico.

The taco originates before the appearance of the Spanish in Mexico in the year 1905. There is anthropological proof that the indigenous individuals living in the lake district of the Valley of Mexico generally ate tacos loaded up with fish. Tacos are now famous everywhere in the world especially in the countries that are situated near Mexico.

Heavenly and notable, the tacos frame part of the social and gastronomic variety of Mexico. The taco has a mind-blowing assortment that suits a wide range of tastes, and it is a paradise for the individuals who cannot digest gluten. Nearly everything in Mexico begins with corn.

Currently, tacos are famous as one of the most widely consumed street foods all over the world and mostly in the U.S.A.

Taco eating competitions are held among individuals, and chefs are trying to bring innovation in the present variety of taco dishes in the world. Mexico has spread its roots deep down across the globe with its amazing and mouthwatering food variety.

The Mexican foods have been famous for a while now, but tacos are the ones that stand out from any other Mexican food. In this cookbook, we will discuss the most of the healthy and yummy recipes related to Mexican Tacos. You will find 77 recipes that consist of breakfast, lunch, dinner, snacks, and vegetarian recipes that you can easily make at your home. Preparing healthy, spicy, and extremely fresh Mexican tacos will not be a problem anymore.

Chapter 1: Welcome to the World of Mexican Taco Breakfast Recipes

The Mexican taco recipes contain amazing, yummy, and healthy breakfast recipes that you can make at home. Following are some of the amazing breakfast taco recipes you can follow:

1.1 Authentic Mexican Breakfast Taco

Cooking Time: 10 minutes

Serving Size: 4

Ingredients:
- Salt, half tsp.
- Salsa, half cup
- Eggs, six

- Corn tortillas, eight
- Milk, a quarter cup
- Chorizo sausage, six ounces
- Hot pepper sauce, half tsp.
- Black pepper half tsp.
- Shredded Monterey jack cheese, half cup

Instructions:
1. Cook the sausage until evenly brown.
2. In a bowl, whisk together the eggs, milk, salt and pepper.
3. Cook the eggs until they turn firm.
4. Add the sausage, and continue cooking for few minutes.
5. Meanwhile, warm tortillas for about forty-five seconds per side in the other skillet, so they are hot and crispy on the edges, but still pliable.
6. Sprinkle a little shredded cheese onto each tortilla while it is still hot.
7. Top with some of the scrambled egg and sausage, and then add hot pepper sauce as well as salsa according to your preference.
8. Your meal is ready to be served.

1.2 Tex-Mex Breakfast Taco

Cooking Time: 15 minutes

Serving Size: 8

Ingredients:

- Jalapeño, one to two
- Tomatoes, two
- Eggs, four
- Red potatoes, two to three
- Freshly chopped parsley and cilantro, two tbsp.
- Salt and pepper to taste
- Onion, half
- Tortillas, eight
- Shredded cheese, half cup
- Breakfast sausage, one roll

Instructions:
1. Add a little olive oil in the pan.
2. Cut the tomatoes, jalapenos, onions, and cilantro.
3. Cook the Smithfield Breakfast Sausage per package instructions.
4. Add the beaten eggs and scramble, set aside.
5. Chop the potatoes into small cubes and cook with a little bit of olive oil, garlic, salt and pepper until they are slightly crispy.
6. Heat the tortilla in a frying pan and add the shredded cheese.
7. Combine the potatoes, eggs, and sausage and mix well.
8. Serve your dish with fresh salsa.

1.3 Chorizo and Egg Breakfast Taco

Cooking Time: 20 minutes

Serving Size: 12

Ingredients:
- Avocado, one
- Salt, half tsp.
- Black pepper, half tsp.
- Egg, twelve
- Milk, six tbsp.
- Cotija cheese, four tbsp.
- Tomatoes, one cup
- Tortillas, twelve
- Hot sauce, as preferred
- Breakfast sausage, one roll
- Cilantro leaves, a quarter cup

Instructions:
1. Cook the egg in a scrambled form.
2. Mix the rest of the things together.
3. Lightly fry the tortilla bread and then arrange all the mixture on the tortillas.
4. Your dish is ready to be served.

1.4 Migas Breakfast Taco

Cooking Time: 20 minutes

Serving Size. 6

Ingredients:
- Avocado, one
- Salt, half tsp.

- Black pepper, half tsp.
- Egg, six
- Tortilla chips, one cup
- Salsa, one cup
- Pepper jack cheese, one cup
- Onion, half cup
- Tortillas, six
- Poblano pepper, one
- Cilantro leaves, a quarter cup

Instructions:
1. Add vegetable oil in a pan.
2. Add the onions, eggs, salt, pepper, poblano pepper, and cilantro.
3. Add the avocados and cook for ten minutes.
4. Add the cheese and lightly fry the tortillas.
5. Arrange all the things in the tortillas and add the crushed tortilla chips on top.
6. Your dish is ready to be served.

1.5 Mexican Street Taco

Cooking Time: 15 minutes

Serving Size: 6

Ingredients:
- Canola oil, two tbsp.
- Chili powder, two tsp.
- Soy sauce, two tbsp.

- Dried oregano, one tsp.
- Beef steak, one and a half pounds
- Minced garlic, three
- Onion, half cup
- Cilantro, half cup
- Ground cumin, one tsp.
- Tortillas, twelve

Instructions:
1. Add all the spices and oil on the steak.
2. Grill the steak and then cut into slices.
3. Lightly fry the tortilla bread and line the steak slices.
4. Your dish is ready to be served.

1.6 Mexican Taco Breakfast Burrito

Cooking Time: 15 minutes

Serving Size: 4

Ingredients:
- Refried beans, one cup
- Cooked ground beef, one pound
- Scrambled eggs, eight
- Taco seasoning, one tsp.
- Onion, one
- Minced garlic, three
- Mixed cheese, one cup
- Avocado, one

- Jalapeno, one
- Tortillas, four
- Tomatoes, one

Instructions:

1. In the center of each tortilla, spread the refried beans, add the ground beef, the scrambled eggs, add the taco seasoning, some cheese, and tomato pieces, jalapeno, and avocado.
2. Fold in the two sides and roll up tightly.
3. Lightly fry the burrito.
4. Serve with hot sauce.

1.7 Quick Breakfast Taco

Cooking Time: 15 minutes

Serving Size: 1

Ingredients:

- Shredded cheddar cheese, two tbsp.
- Salsa, one tbsp.
- Eggs, two
- Tortillas, two

Instructions:

1. Cook the egg and add cheddar cheese into it.
2. Arrange the taco by adding the egg mixture and salsa.
3. Your dish is ready to be served.

1.8 Scrambled Egg Taco

Cooking Time: 10 minutes

Serving Size: 2

Ingredients:
- Unsalted butter, one tbsp.
- Salsa, one tbsp.
- Eggs, four
- Corn tortillas, four
- Cilantro, two tbsp.
- Monetary Jack cheese, half cup
- Avocado, one

Instructions:
1. Cook the egg and keep stirring.
2. Add the rest of the ingredients and warm the corn tortillas.
3. Arrange the scrambled egg in the tortillas.
4. Garnish with cilantro.
5. Your dish is ready to be served.

1.9 Breakfast Taco with Avocado Cream

Cooking Time: 10 minutes

Serving Size: 8

Ingredients:
- Smoked paprika, one tbsp.
- Salt and pepper to taste

- Eggs, eight
- Corn tortillas, eight
- Cilantro, two tbsp.
- Cumin, one tsp.
- Black beans, half cup
- Mushrooms, one cup
- Red bell pepper, one
- Olive oil, one tbsp.
- Avocado slices, as required
- Salsa, as required
- Jalapeno slices, half cup
- Monetary Jack cheese, half cup
- Avocado cream, one cup

Instructions:
1. Cook the eggs; add the ingredients into the mixture.
2. Arrange the egg mixture on the tortillas.
3. Add the avocado cream on top of it, place jalapeno slices, avocado slices and salsa on top.
4. Your dish is ready to be served.

1.10 Chorizo and Potato Breakfast Taco

Cooking Time: 20 minutes

Serving Size: 4

Ingredients:
- Mexican chorizo, half pound
- Salt and pepper to taste

- Eggs, four
- Corn tortillas, four
- Cilantro, two tbsp.
- Serrano pepper, one
- Sour cream, half cup
- Salsa, one cup
- Red bell pepper, one
- Olive oil, one tbsp.
- Salsa, as required
- Potatoes, two
- Monetary Jack cheese, half cup

Instructions:
1. Add onion and cook until they turn soft.
2. Then add the chorizo and potatoes.
3. Let them cook properly for fifteen minutes.
4. Add the rest of the ingredients including the cheese.
5. Arrange all the mixture on the tortillas.
6. Garnish it with a little cilantro on top.
7. Your dish is ready to be served.

1.11 Pancake Breakfast Taco

Cooking Time: 10 minutes

Serving Size: 3

Ingredients:
- Eggs, two

- Milk, one cup
- Brown sugar, two tbsp.
- Bisquick, one and a half cup
- Chopped chives, one tbsp.
- Bacon, six strips
- Salt and pepper to taste

Instructions:
1. Cook the egg, add chopped chives, salt, and pepper.
2. Mix one egg, brown sugar, bisquick, and milk in a bowl.
3. Cook the pan cakes.
4. Arrange the pancakes; add the cooked eggs, and bacon on top.
5. Your dish is ready to be served.

1.12 Paleo Breakfast Taco

Cooking Time: 15 minutes

Serving Size: 2

Ingredients:
- Egg, six
- Salsa, half cup
- Avocado oil, two tsp.
- Lime, one
- Tortillas, two
- Bacon, four strips
- Chopped cilantro, two tbsp.

- Chopped avocado, one
- Salt and pepper to taste

Instructions:
1. Add the avocado oil in a pan.
2. Add the egg and mix it until it gets firm.
3. Add salt and pepper.
4. Arrange the tortillas; add the egg, cilantro, chopped avocado, salsa, and lime on top of the eggs.
5. Your dish is ready to be served.

Chapter 2: Mexican Taco Lunch Recipes

Mexican Taco lunch recipes are amazing, healthy and you will love making them on your own. Following are some amazing recipes below:

2.1 Smoky Pork and Black Bean Taco

Cooking Time: 15 minutes

Serving Size: 4

Ingredients:

- Chopped red onion, half
- Shredded ice berg lettuce, half
- Minced pork meat, one pound

- Barbeque sauce, five tbsp.
- Black beans, one cup
- Taco shells, eight
- Ground cumin and paprika two tsp.
- Passata, half cup
- Sour cream, as required
- Chopped avocado, one
- Chopped coriander, a bunch

Instructions:
1. Heat the oil in a large frying pan, add the onion.
2. Cook for five minutes until softened.
3. Sprinkle over the spices and cook for a while.
4. Add the mince, and add the passata and barbecue sauce into the pan.
5. Increase the heat and add the beans.
6. Use the pork and bean mix to fill the tacos.
7. Top with slices of avocado, shredded iceberg lettuce and sour cream.

2.2 Grilled Salmon Tacos

Cooking Time: 15 minutes

Serving Size: 4

Ingredients:
- Chopped red onion, half
- Salmon filet one pound
- Olive oil, five tbsp.

- Taco shells, eight
- Taco seasoning, two tbsp.
- Chopped avocado, one
- Chopped coriander, a bunch
- Salt and pepper to taste

Instructions:
1. Add the olive oil, salt, pepper, and taco seasoning on the salmon filet.
2. Grill the filet for ten minutes and then slice it up.
3. Heat the taco shells and start filling it with salmon filet slices, red onions, avocado slices and coriander on top.
4. Your dish is ready to be served.

2.3 Chipotle Chicken Tacos

Cooking Time: 15 minutes

Serving Size: 4

Ingredients:
- Chopped red onion, half
- Chicken breast filet, one pound
- Olive oil, five tbsp.
- Taco shells, eight
- Chipotle sauce, two tbsp.
- Chopped avocado, one
- Chopped cilantro, a bunch
- Salt and pepper to taste

Instructions:

1. Add the olive oil, salt, and pepper on the chicken filet.
2. Grill the filet for ten minutes and then slice it up.
3. Heat the taco shells and start filling it with chicken slices, chipotle sauce, red onions, avocado slices and cilantro on top.
4. Your dish is ready to be served.

2.4 Meatball Tacos

Cooking Time: 20 minutes

Serving Size: 4

Ingredients:

- Chopped red onion, half
- Chicken mince, one pound
- Olive oil, five tbsp.
- Taco shells, eight
- Barbeque sauce, two tbsp.
- Chopped avocado, one
- Chopped cilantro, a bunch
- Salt and pepper to taste
- Red paprika powder, two tsp.

Instructions:

1. Add the mince in a bowl with the salt, red paprika, and pepper and mix.
2. Make balls and cook it for ten minutes until done.
3. Now arrange your tacos, add meatballs, barbeque sauce, avocado, onion and cilantro on top.

4. Your dish is ready to be served.

2.5 Prawn Tacos

Cooking Time: 15 minutes

Serving Size: 4

Ingredients:

- Chopped red onion, half
- Prawns, one pound
- Olive oil, five tbsp.
- Taco shells, eight
- Taco seasoning, two tbsp.
- Chopped avocado, one
- Chopped cilantro, a bunch
- Salsa, half cup
- Salt and pepper to taste

Instructions:

1. Add the olive oil, salt, pepper, and taco seasoning on the prawns.
2. Cook the prawns for ten minutes.
3. Heat the taco shells and start filling it with prawns, red onions, avocado slices and cilantro on top.
4. Your dish is ready to be served.

2.6 Mexican Pulled Pork Tacos

Cooking Time: six hours

Serving Size: 4

Ingredients:
- Chopped red onion, half
- Pork shoulder, two pounds
- Olive oil, five tbsp.
- Taco shells, eight
- Chopped avocado, one
- Chopped cilantro, a bunch
- Salsa, half cup
- Oregano, two tsp.
- Cumin, two tbsp.
- Salt and pepper to taste

Instructions:
1. Add the oregano, salt, cumin, pepper, and pork shoulder.
2. Cook for six hours straight.
3. Shred the pork slices and arrange the tacos.
4. Add the rest of the ingredients on top.
5. Your dish is ready to be served.

2.7 Speedy Beef Tacos

Cooking Time: 30 minutes

Serving Size: 4

Ingredients:
- Tomatoes, eight
- Beef, one pound

- Guacamole, eight tbsp.
- Sweetcorn, one cup
- Taco shells, eight
- Taco seasoning, two tsp.
- Salt and pepper to taste
- Lettuce, as required

Instructions:

1. Cook the beef in the taco seasoning, salt, and pepper.
2. Heat the taco shells and add the beef slices along with tomatoes, guacamole, lettuce and sweetcorn.
3. Your dish is ready to be served.

2.8 Chipotle Cod Tacos

Cooking Time: 12 minutes

Serving Size: 2

Ingredients:

- Cod, two
- Lime slaw, two tbsp.
- Salsa, one cup
- Taco shells, eight
- Chipotle paste, two tsp.
- Salt and pepper to taste
- Lettuce, as required

Instructions:

1. Slice the cod and mix with the chipotle paste, lime juice and olive oil.

2. Leave to marinate while you make the slaw.
3. Mix all the slaw ingredients together, season and set aside.
4. Put the cod on a baking tray and roast for ten minutes.
5. Heat the taco shells properly.
6. Arrange all the things in the taco shell and serve immediately.

2.9 Tex-Mex Beef Tacos

Cooking Time: 20 minutes

Serving Size: 6

Ingredients:
- Beef mince, one pound
- Salt and pepper as required
- Vegetable oil two tbsp.
- Oregano, two tsp.
- Garlic, one
- Taco shells, six
- Avocado, one
- Red onions, one
- Cilantro, as required

Instructions:
1. Heat a large frying pan, and then cook the mince.
2. Season with salt and pepper.
3. Add oil to the pan and fry the garlic, oregano and spices for a few minutes.

4. Heat the taco shells.
5. Add cilantro, avocado slices and red onion on top.
6. Your dish is ready to be served.

2.10 Turkey Chili and Rice Tacos

Cooking Time: 35 minutes

Serving Size: 8

Ingredients:
- Turkey mince, one pound
- Salt and pepper as required
- Vegetable oil, two tbsp.
- Rice, one cup
- Cooked red beans, half cup
- Sweetcorn, half cup
- Taco shells, eight
- Avocado, one
- Red onions, one
- Coriander, as required

Instructions:
1. Add the mince in a pan and cook until browned.
2. Add in the rice and beans, and mix well, then add the stock.
3. Cover and simmer for twenty minutes until the rice is tender, then stir in the sweetcorn and scatter over the coriander.
4. Heat the taco shells.

5. Add the cooked mixture, and rest of the ingredients just before serving in the taco shells.
6. Your dish is ready to be served.

2.11 Fish Finger Tacos

Cooking Time: 12 minutes

Serving Size: 10

Ingredients:
- Finger fish, one pack
- Salt and pepper as required
- Vegetable oil, two tbsp.
- Avocado, one
- Salsa, one cup
- Cilantro, as required
- Taco shells, eight

Instructions:
1. Cook the fish fingers.
2. Heat the taco shells.
3. Arrange all the ingredients in the taco shells.
4. Your dish is ready to be served.

2.12 Fish Tacos with Chili Cream and Jalapeño Salsa

Cooking Time: 12 minutes

Serving Size: 10

Ingredients:

- Finger fish, one pack
- Salt and pepper as required
- Vegetable oil, two tbsp.
- Avocado, one
- Chili cream, ten tbsp.
- Jalapeno salsa, one cup
- Cilantro, as required
- Taco shells, eight

Instructions:

1. Cook the finger fish according to the pack instructions.
2. Heat the tacos.
3. Add the finger fish, chili cream, jalapeno salsa, avocado, and cilantro on top.
4. Your dish is ready to be served.

2.13 Crispy Chicken and Pineapple Tacos

Cooking Time: 10 minutes

Serving Size: 5

Ingredients:

- Chicken breast, one pound
- Salt and pepper as required
- Vegetable oil, two tbsp.
- Avocado, one
- Pineapple slices, one cup
- Cilantro, as required

- Taco shells, eight

Instructions:
1. Cook the chicken breast in the oil and add salt and pepper to it.
2. Slice up the chicken pieces and heat the taco shells.
3. Arrange all the ingredients in the taco shells.
4. Your dish is ready to be served.

2.14 Crab and Avocado Tacos

Cooking Time: 10 minutes

Serving Size: 4

Ingredients:
- Crab meat, one pound
- Salt and pepper as required
- Vegetable oil, two tbsp.
- Avocado, one
- Cilantro, as required
- Taco shells, eight

Instructions:
1. Cook the crab meat in the oil and add salt and pepper to it.
2. Heat up the taco shells.
3. Arrange all the ingredients in the taco shells.
4. Your dish is ready to be served.

2.15 BBQ Bean Tacos

Cooking Time: 30 minutes

Serving Size: 4

Ingredients:

- Black beans, one cup
- Salt and pepper as required
- Vegetable oil, two tbsp.
- Avocado, one
- Vegetable stock, half cup
- Barbeque sauce, two tbsp.
- Cilantro, as required
- Taco shells, eight
- Sour cream, as required

Instructions:

1. Cook the red beans in oil, vegetable stock, and barbeque sauce for ten to fifteen minutes.
2. Arrange the beans, and rest of the ingredients in the taco shells.
3. Your dish is ready to be served.

Chapter 3: Mexican Taco Dinner Recipes

Mexico is a very diverse food cultured nation. The dinner recipes are amazing and extremely delicious to consume. Following are some amazing dinner taco recipes that you can make at home:

3.1 Kingfish Ceviche Tacos

Cooking Time: 15 minutes

Serving Size: 4

Ingredients:
- Kingfish Ceviche, one pound
- Salt and chili as required
- Vegetable oil, two tbsp.
- Lime juice, two tsp.
- Sugar, one tsp.

- Avocado, one
- Cilantro, as required
- Tortillas, four

Instructions:

1. Place lime juice, sugar, salt and chili in a bowl and stir until sugar and salt dissolve.
2. Add kingfish, gently stir to coat.
3. Cook the fish until done.
4. Drain ceviche and serve with tortillas, and all the toppings.

3.2 Taco Rice with Grilled Chicken and Green Chili Salsa

Cooking Time: 25 minutes

Serving Size: 4

Ingredients:

- Chicken, one pound
- Salt and pepper as required
- Vegetable oil, two tbsp.
- Lime juice, two tsp.
- Green chili salsa, one cup
- Cooked rice, one cup
- Cilantro, two tbsp.
- Taco shells, eight

Instructions:
1. Cook the chicken by adding the seasonings.
2. Slice the chicken once it is cooked properly.
3. Now arrange the chicken slices on the taco shells, add the cooked rice, green chili salsa, and cilantro.
4. Your dish is ready to be served.

3.3 Chicken Tacos with Charred Corn

Cooking Time: 25 minutes

Serving Size: 4

Ingredients:
- Chicken, one pound
- Salt and pepper as required
- Vegetable oil, two tbsp.
- Lime juice, two tsp.
- Charred corns, one cup
- Cilantro, two tbsp.
- Sour cream, as required
- Taco shells, eight

Instructions:
1. Cook the chicken by adding the seasonings.
2. Slice the chicken once it is cooked properly.
3. Now arrange the chicken slices on the taco shells, add the corns, sour cream, and cilantro on top.
4. Your dish is ready to be served.

3.4 Tacos de Carne Asada

Cooking Time: 25 minutes

Serving Size: 4

Ingredients:
- Chicken, one pound
- Salt and pepper as required
- Vegetable oil, two tbsp.
- Lime juice, two tsp.
- Shredded cheese, one cup
- Pico de Gallo, one cup
- Mojo, half cup
- Cilantro, two tbsp.
- Sour cream, as required
- Taco shells, eight

Instructions:
1. Cook the chicken breast in oil.
2. Add salt and pepper on top.
3. Slice the chicken when done, and heat the taco shells.
4. Now, arrange the chicken on the taco shells, add a tbsp. of mojo, sour cream, Pico de Gallo and shredded cheese on top.
5. Grill the tacos for two minutes, add cilantro.
6. Your dish is ready to be served.

3.5 Kingfish Ceviche Tacos with Tabasco

Cooking Time: 15 minutes

Serving Size: 4

Ingredients:
- Kingfish Ceviche, one pound
- Salt and chili as required
- Vegetable oil, two tbsp.
- Lime juice, two tsp.
- Sugar, one tsp.
- Avocado, one
- Tabasco, two tbsp.
- Cilantro, as required
- Tortillas, four

Instructions:
1. Place lime juice, sugar, salt and chili in a bowl and stir until sugar and salt dissolve.
2. Add tabasco and kingfish, gently stir to coat.
3. Cook the fish until done.
4. Drain ceviche, slice up the fish.
5. Serve with tortillas, and add all the rest ingredients on top.

3.6 Quick Chicken Tacos with Homemade Hot Sauce

Cooking Time: 15 minutes

Serving Size: 4

Ingredients:

- Chicken breast, one pound
- Tomato sauce, two tbsp.
- Vinegar, two tbsp.
- Worcestershire sauce, one tbsp.
- Mustard paste, one tbsp.
- Chili sauce, two tsp.
- Sugar, one tsp.
- Avocado, one
- Salsa, half cup
- Cilantro, as required
- Tortillas, four

Instructions:

1. Mix the tomato sauce, sugar, vinegar, Worcestershire, mustard and chili in a saucepan over medium heat.
2. Bring to a simmer and cook for a few minutes until the sugar is dissolved and sauce is sticky.
3. Cook the chicken, and then slice it up.
4. Now add the filling in the taco shells, add the sauce and rest of the toppings.
5. Your dish is ready to be served.

3.7 Slow Cooker Green Chili Chicken Tacos

Cooking Time: one hour

Serving Size: 4

Ingredients:
- Chicken breast, one pound
- Green chili paste, two tsp.
- Vegetable stock, two cups
- Avocado, one
- Salsa, half cup
- Cilantro, as required
- Tortillas, four

Instructions:
1. Cook the chicken in the stock and green chili paste for fifty minutes.
2. Now serve with tortillas, avocado slices, salsa, and add cilantro on top.
3. Your dish is ready to be served.

3.8 Chicken and Avocado Taco with Creamy Cilantro Sauce

Cooking Time: 15 minutes

Serving Size: 4

Ingredients:
- Chicken breast, one pound
- Cilantro sauce, four tbsp.
- Avocado, one
- Salsa, half cup
- Cilantro, as required

- Taco shells, four

Instructions:
1. Cook the chicken breast and then slice it up.
2. Now heat the taco shells and add chicken, avocado slices and creamy cilantro sauce on top.
3. Add cilantro in the end.
4. Your dish is ready to be served.

3.9 Blackened Salmon Tacos

Cooking Time: 15 minutes

Serving Size: 4

Ingredients:
- Salmon filet, one pound
- Mix spice, two tbsp.
- Olive oil, two tbsp.
- Avocado, one
- Salsa, half cup
- Cilantro, as required
- Taco shells, four

Instructions:
1. Cook the salmon filet in the mix spice and olive oil.
2. Now slice it up and add it in the heated taco shells.
3. Add the rest of the ingredients on top.
4. Your dish is ready to be served.

3.10 Spicy Shrimp Tacos with Creamy Sirarcha Sauce and Cilantro Lime Slaw

Cooking Time: 20 minutes

Serving Size: 4

Ingredients:
- Shrimp, one pound
- Paprika, two tbsp.
- Olive oil, two tbsp.
- Avocado, one
- Salsa, half cup
- Creamy sirarcha sauce, four tbsp.
- Cilantro lime slaw, four tbsp.
- Cilantro, as required
- Taco shells, four

Instructions:
1. Add the olive oil, shrimps, and paprika in a bowl.
2. Grill the shrimps until they are done.
3. Heat the taco shells; add the shrimps, creamy sirarcha sauce, cilantro lime slaw and cilantro on top.
4. Your dish is ready to be served.

3.11 Roasted Cauliflower Tacos

Cooking Time: 15 minutes

Serving Size: 4

Ingredients:

- Cauliflower, two cups
- Mix spice, two tbsp.
- Olive oil, two tbsp.
- Salsa, half cup
- Cilantro, as required
- Taco shells, four

Instructions:

1. Roast the cauliflower by adding the mix spice and olive oil.
2. Roast for ten minutes.
3. Add the cauliflower in the taco shells; add salsa, and cilantro on top.
4. Your dish is ready to be served.

3.12 Spicy Chicken and Kidney Bean Tacos

Cooking Time: 20 minutes

Serving Size: 4

Ingredients:

- Kidney beans, one cup
- Chicken breast, one pound
- Mix spice, two tbsp.
- Olive oil, two tbsp.
- Salsa, half cup
- Sour cream, four tbsp.
- Cilantro, as required
- Taco shells, four

- Chicken stock, half cup

Instructions:
1. Cook the chicken and red beans in the chicken stock.
2. Add the mix spice into it and olive oil.
3. Heat the taco shells; add the chicken and red bean mixture into it.
4. Top with sour cream, salsa, and cilantro.
5. Your dish is ready to be served.

3.13 Pork Tacos with Dill and Apple Coleslaw

Cooking Time: 20 minutes

Serving Size: 4

Ingredients:
- Apple chunks, one cup
- Pork meat, one pound
- Salt and pepper to taste
- Olive oil, two tbsp.
- Dill, one tbsp.
- Lime juice, two tbsp.
- Cilantro, as required
- Taco shells, four

Instructions:
1. Cook the pork meat in olive oil for ten minutes.
2. Now mix the apple chunks, dill, salt, pepper, lime juice and cilantro in a bowl.

3. Heat the taco shells.
4. Add the pork meat and apple and dill coleslaw on top.
5. Your dish is ready to be served.

3.14 Taco Pull Apart

Cooking Time: 45 minutes

Serving Size: 4

Ingredients:
- Onion, one
- Crushed garlic, one
- Red chili, one
- Beef mince, one pound
- Salt and pepper to taste
- Olive oil, two tbsp.
- Taco spice mix, two tbsp.
- Cilantro, as required
- Tortillas, eight
- Grated cheese, one cup
- Cilantro, as required

Instructions:
1. In a large frying pan heat the olive oil and then add the diced onion.
2. Next add the crushed garlic and diced red chili and fry for another minute.
3. Finally add the beef mince and turn the heat up.

4. Add the taco spice mix and some seasoning and continue to fry the mince.
5. Add the mixture in each tortilla.
6. Take each tortilla and neatly trim the edges so they are square.
7. Add grated cheese on top.
8. Bake them for thirty minutes.
9. Add cilantro on top and serve immediately.

3.15 Cheesy Shell Tacos

Cooking Time: 25 minutes

Serving Size: 4

Ingredients:
- Onion, one
- Crushed garlic, one
- Red chili, one
- Beef mince, one pound
- Salt and pepper to taste
- Olive oil, two tbsp.
- Taco spice mix, two tbsp.
- Cilantro, as required
- Grated cheddar cheese, two cups

Instructions:
1. Melt the cheese in the form of round shapes and cook it in the form of tacos.
2. Cook the beef mince, onions, taco mix, and spices.

3. Add the beef mixture, and rest of the ingredients in the cheese taco shells.
4. Your dish is ready to be served.

Chapter 4: Mexican Taco Snack Recipes

Mexican taco snacks are diverse and very tasty in flavor. Following are some easy snack recipes that you can make at home:

4.1 Corn and Cottage Cheese Tacos

Cooking Time: 25 minutes

Serving Size: 4

Ingredients:
- Onion, one
- Cottage cheese, one cup
- Corn kernels, one cup
- Salt and pepper to taste
- Olive oil, two tbsp.
- Taco spice mix, two tbsp.

- Cilantro, as required
- Green chili sauce, two tbsp.
- Taco shells, eight
- Avocado, one

Instructions:

1. Mix the cottage cheese crumbs, corn kernels, salt, pepper, taco spice mix in a bowl.
2. Heat the taco shells in an oven.
3. Add the cottage cheese and corn mixture into the taco shells.
4. Add the green chili sauce on top with onion, avocado slices, and cilantro on top.
5. Your dish is ready to be served.

4.2 Mini Chicken Taco Cups

Cooking Time: 25 minutes

Serving Size: 4

Ingredients:

- Salsa, one cup
- Cotija cheese, one cup
- Shredded chicken, one cup
- Salt and pepper to taste
- Olive oil, two tbsp.
- Refried beans, one cup
- Cilantro, as required
- Cumin, one tsp.

- Garlic powder, one tsp.
- Tortilla sheets, eight

Instructions:
1. Preheat the oven to 425 degrees.
2. Add olive oil in the bottom of each muffin cup.
3. Press the tortilla into the cup.
4. Bake the tortillas for five minutes until golden brown.
5. Place the shredded chicken in a bowl and mix with two tablespoons of salsa.
6. Mix the refried beans, with two tablespoons of salsa, cumin, and garlic powder.
7. Place a teaspoon of the refried bean filling in the bottom of each taco shell.
8. Place one tablespoon of shredded chicken and top with cotija cheese crumbles.
9. Bake the taco cups for ten minutes or until the cheese is melted.
10. Add cilantro on top and serve immediately.

4.3 Taco Bites

Cooking Time: 15 minutes

Serving Size: 4

Ingredients:
- Pico de Galo, one cup
- Mix cheese, one cup
- Shredded chicken, one cup
- Salt and pepper to taste

- Olive oil, two tbsp.
- Refried beans, one cup
- Cilantro, as required
- Tortilla sheets, eight

Instructions:

1. In a muffin tray, add the tortilla sheets and then a layer of refried beans.
2. Next add a little cheese on top and then a layer of the shredded chicken.
3. In the end add cheese again and bake for ten minutes.
4. Next add a spoon of Pico de Galo on top and some cilantro leaves.
5. Your dish is ready to be served.

4.4 Mini Beef and Cheese Tacos

Cooking Time: 25 minutes

Serving Size: 4

Ingredients:

- Salsa, one cup
- Mix cheese, one cup
- Beef, one cup
- Salt and pepper to taste
- Taco seasoning, one tsp.
- Basil leaf, as required
- Olive oil, two tbsp.
- Cilantro, as required

- Cumin, one tsp.
- Garlic powder, one tsp.
- Taco shells, small sized, eight to twelve

Instructions:
1. Cook the beef mince in oil, add the spices into it.
2. When cooked, remove from the stove.
3. Heat the taco shells.
4. Now in the taco shells add the beef mixture and add cheese on top.
5. Bake for five minutes.
6. Now add the salsa and cilantro on top.
7. Your dish is ready to be served.

4.5 Taco Pinwheels

Cooking Time: 15 minutes

Serving Size: 6

Ingredients:
- Taco seasoning, one tsp.
- Shredded chicken, one cup
- Bell peppers, one cup
- Salt and pepper to taste
- Cheddar cheese, one cup
- Cilantro, as required
- Cream cheese, one cup
- Tortilla sheets, eight

Instructions:

1. In a large bowl, mix together the cream cheese, taco seasoning and cheddar cheese until well combined.
2. Add the chicken, bell peppers and cilantro into the cream cheese mixture and stir until combined.
3. Lay one of the tortillas flat on a cutting board and spread some of the chicken mixture all over the tortilla.
4. Roll up tightly.
5. Repeat the process with the remaining tortillas.
6. Place the tortilla rolls on a plate and cover with plastic wrap.
7. Chill for at least one hour or up to one day.
8. Slice up the tortilla rolls, and serve the tortilla pinwheels with your preferred toppings.

4.6 Mini Shrimp Tacos

Cooking Time: 20 minutes

Serving Size: 6

Ingredients:

- Beef mince, one pound
- Salt and pepper as required
- Vegetable oil two tbsp.
- Oregano, two tsp.
- Garlic, one
- Mini taco shells, twelve
- Avocado, one
- Red onions, one

- Cilantro, as required

Instructions:
1. Heat a large frying pan, and then cook the shrimps.
2. Season with salt and pepper.
3. Add the oil to the pan and fry the garlic, oregano and spices for a few minutes.
4. Heat the taco shells.
5. Add cilantro, avocado slices and red onion on top.
6. Your dish is ready to be served.

4.7 Taco Wanton Cups

Ingredients:
- Pico de Galo, one cup
- Mix cheese, one cup
- Shredded chicken, one cup
- Salt and pepper to taste
- Olive oil, two tbsp.
- Refried beans, one cup
- Cilantro, as required
- Wonton sheets, eight

Instructions:
1. In a muffin tray, add the wonton sheets and then a layer of refried beans.
2. Next add a little cheese on top and then a layer of the shredded chicken.
3. In the end add cheese again and bake for ten minutes.

4. Next add a spoon of Pico de Galo on top and some cilantro leaves.
5. Your dish is ready to be served.

4.8 Turkey Taco Cups

Cooking Time: 25 minutes

Serving Size: 4

Ingredients:
- Salsa, one cup
- Cotija cheese, one cup
- Shredded turkey, one cup
- Salt and pepper to taste
- Olive oil, two tbsp.
- Refried beans, one cup
- Cilantro, as required
- Cumin, one tsp.
- Garlic powder, one tsp.
- Tortilla sheets, eight

Instructions:
1. Preheat the oven to 425 degrees.
2. Add olive oil in the bottom of each muffin cup.
3. Press the tortilla into the cup.
4. Bake the tortillas for five minutes until golden brown.
5. Place the shredded turkey a bowl and mix with two tablespoons of salsa.

6. Mix the refried beans, with two tablespoons of salsa, cumin, and garlic powder.
7. Place a teaspoon of the refried bean filling in the bottom of each taco shell.
8. Place one tablespoon of shredded turkey and top with cotija cheese crumbles.
9. Bake the taco cups for ten minutes or until the cheese is melted.
10. Add cilantro on top and serve immediately.

Instructions:

4.9 Shrimp Taco Bites

Cooking Time: 15 minutes

Serving Size: 4

Ingredients:

- Pico de Galo, one cup
- Mix cheese, one cup
- Grilled shrimps, half pound
- Salt and pepper to taste
- Olive oil, two tbsp.
- Refried beans, one cup
- Cilantro, as required
- Tortilla sheets, eight

Instructions:

1. In a muffin tray, add the tortilla sheets and then a layer of refried beans.
2. Next add a little cheese on top and then a shrimp.

3. In the end add cheese again and bake for ten minutes.
4. Next add a spoon of Pico de Galo on top and some cilantro leaves.
5. Your dish is ready to be served.

4.10 Taco Cupcakes

Cooking Time: 20 minutes

Serving Size: 18

Ingredients:
- Wonton wrapper, as required
- Mix shredded cheese, one cup
- Minced beef, one pound
- Salt and pepper to taste
- Olive oil, two tbsp.
- Refried beans, one cup
- Cilantro, as required
- Taco seasoning, two tsp.
- Tortilla chips, as required
- Avocado, one
- Sour cream, as required

Instructions:
1. Preheat the oven.
2. Spray the muffin cups with cooking spray.
3. Cook the beef in a skillet.
4. Add the taco seasoning mix and cook for five minutes.

5. Place one wonton wrapper in the bottom of each muffin cup.
6. Layer some of the refried beans on top of each wonton.
7. Crush one tortilla chip on top of the beans.
8. Add the taco meat and some of the shredded cheese.
9. Bake for ten minutes until the cheese melts.
10. Add your favorite toppings on it.
11. Your dish is ready to be served.

4.11 Tacos Dorados

Cooking Time: 25 minutes

Serving Size: 4

Ingredients:
- Ground beef, one pound
- Sour cream, as required
- Chili powder, one tsp.
- Cumin powder, one tsp.
- Garlic powder, one tsp.
- Onion, one
- Tomatoes, one cup
- Salt and pepper to taste
- Olive oil, two tbsp.
- Cheddar cheese, half cup
- Mozzarella cheese, half cup
- Cilantro, as required
- Tortilla sheets, eight

Instructions:

1. In a large pan, add the onion and oil and let it cook.
2. Add the ground beef and then all the spices, let it cook for five minutes.
3. Now add the tomatoes.
4. Place the mixture on the tortilla sheets, add sour cream and roll it.
5. Place the rolled tortillas in a baking dish and add cheese on top.
6. Now let it bake for five minutes until the cheese melts.
7. Your dish is ready to be served.

4.12 Taco Fries

Cooking Time: 15 minutes

Serving Size: 4

Ingredients:

- Salsa, one cup
- Mix cheese, one cup
- Shredded chicken, one cup
- Salt and pepper to taste
- Olive oil, two tbsp.
- Cilantro, as required
- Taco seasoning, one tsp.
- Potatoes, eight

Instructions:

1. Cut the potatoes and fry it properly.

2. Add the taco seasoning on top and mix.
3. Arrange the fries in a plate and add olive oil, salsa, salt, pepper, and cheese and let it bake for five minutes until the cheese melts.
4. Add cilantro on top.
5. Your dish is ready to be served.

4.13 Chicharrons Tacos

Cooking Time: 50 minutes

Serving Size: 4

Ingredients:
- Tomatillo salsa, one cup
- Pork chops, one pound
- Salt and pepper to taste
- Olive oil, two tbsp.
- Cilantro, as required
- Cumin, one tsp.
- Garlic powder, one tsp.
- Tortilla sheets, eight

Instructions:
1. In a large, heavy skillet, add the pork meat, and other spices.
2. Cook over low heat for forty minutes.
3. Transfer the chicharrons to a large saucepan, add the tomatillo salsa.
4. Cook on medium-high heat until the sauce is almost dried up and coats the chicharrons.

5. Add cilantro on top
6. Remove from the heat.
7. Serve immediately with tortillas.

4.14 Rolled Taco Dip

Cooking Time: 30 minutes

Serving Size: 6

Ingredients:
- Cooked chicken, one cup
- Pepper jack cheese, three cups
- Tortilla chips, as required
- Green onions, a quarter cup
- Cumin, two tsp.
- Green salsa, half cup
- Garlic powder, one tsp.
- Lime juice, four tsp.
- Onion powder, one tsp.
- Chili powder, one tsp.
- Salt and pepper as required

Instructions:
1. Mix all the ingredients together in a bowl.
2. Add the mixture into a baking tray and let it bake for twenty to twenty-five minutes.
3. Add some extra cheese on top and bake for extra five minutes.
4. Serve your dip with the tortilla chips and enjoy.

4.15 Tangy Taco Tarts

Cooking Time: 25 minutes

Serving Size: 4

Ingredients:
- Corn kernels, one cup
- Chopped tomatoes, one cup
- Cheddar cheese, one cup
- Salt and pepper to taste
- Olive oil, two tbsp.
- Jalapeno, two
- Green chili paste, one tsp.
- Chili flakes, one tsp.
- Cilantro, as required
- Cumin, one tsp.
- Oregano, one tsp.
- Baked tarts, eight

Instructions:
1. In a pan heat the oil and add chopped bell peppers.
2. Now add corn kernels, jalapeno, green chilies, salt, chili flakes, ground cumin, and oregano into it.
3. Add the chopped tomato into the mixture.
4. Add cheddar cheese, mix for a while and take out in a bowl.

5. Fill the baked tarts with the topping and put some grated cheese on the top.
6. Serve with your proffered dip or sauce.

Chapter 5: Mexican Taco Vegetarian Recipes

Mexican cuisine is mostly composed of carnivorous diet but if you look into the cuisine you may also find the vegetarian recipes that have the similar taste just as the non-vegetarian recipes. Following are some vegetarian recipes that you can follow:

5.1 Vegan Street Tacos

Cooking Time: 45 minutes

Serving Size: 4

Ingredients:

- Mushrooms, one cup
- Walnuts, one cup
- Cumin, one tbsp.
- Tamari, one tbsp.
- Chili powder, one tsp.

- Quinoa, one cup
- Onion, one
- Tomato paste, one tbsp.
- Corn tortillas, four
- Cilantro, as required
- Green bell pepper, one
- Vegetable broth, two cups

Instructions:

1. Cook the quinoa in the vegetable broth.
2. Add tomato paste, onion, green bell pepper, cumin and chili powder into it.
3. Next, add the mushrooms into it and when done remove from the stove.
4. Place the mixture on the corn tortillas; add the walnuts, tamari sauce on top.
5. Garnish with cilantro leaves.
6. Your dish is ready to be served.

5.2 Quinoa Taco Meat

Cooking Time: 40 minutes

Serving Size: 4

Ingredients:

- Sour cream, as required
- Walnuts, one cup
- Cumin, one tbsp.
- Tamari, one tbsp.

- Chili powder, one tsp.
- Quinoa, one cup
- Onion, one
- Tomato paste, one tbsp.
- Corn tortillas, four
- Cilantro, as required
- Green bell pepper, one
- Red bell pepper, one
- Vegetable broth, two cups

Instructions:

1. Cook the quinoa in the vegetable broth.
2. Add tomato paste, onion, green and red bell pepper, cumin and chili powder into it.
3. Place the mixture on the corn tortillas; add the walnuts, tamari sauce or sour cream on top.
4. Garnish with cilantro leaves.
5. Your dish is ready to be served.

5.3 Black Beans and Zucchini Tacos

Cooking Time: 25 minutes

Serving Size: 4

Ingredients:

- Bean stew powder, one tbsp.
- Coriander, one tbsp.
- Salt as required
- Coleslaw, one cup

- Cilantro, as required, pepper, one tsp.
- Cumin powder, one tsp.
- Zucchini, one cup
- Black beans, one cup
- Green onions, half cup
- Paprika, one tsp.
- Oregano, one tsp.
- Tortilla sheets, eight
- Chopped avocado, one

Instructions:

1. Mix the zucchini with the salt, oregano, paprika, coriander, and bean stew powder.
2. Put together the coleslaw, cilantro, and green onions.
3. Season with salt, pepper, and cumin.
4. Add lime juice and mix effectively to make it yummy and flavorful.
5. Add the chopped avocado.
6. Warm the olive oil over medium high heat.
7. Add the zucchini.
8. Cook for approximately five minutes.
9. Add the dark beans and cook until they are ready.
10. Lightly heat tortillas on anything available to you.
11. Fill the tortillas with all the ingredients above.
12. Add cilantro to garnish.
13. Your meal is ready to be served.

5.4 Lentil Tacos

Cooking Time: 45 minutes

Serving Size: 4

Ingredients:
- Brown lentils, one cup
- Paprika, one tsp.
- Cumin powder, one tsp.
- Taco seasoning, one tsp.
- Sour cream, as required.
- Salsa, one cup
- Salt and pepper to taste
- Olive oil, two tbsp.
- Cilantro, as required
- Tortilla sheets, eight
- Vegetable stock, one cup

Instructions:
1. Add all the spices, along with the lentils in a deep pan.
2. Now mix all the spices including the taco mix, and add the vegetable stock.
3. Cook it for thirty minutes until the lentils are cooked properly.
4. Now move the tortillas in a pan.
5. Place the lentils, a little sour cream, salsa, and a few leaves of cilantro on top.
6. Roll the tortilla sheets.

7. You can add any other topping if you like; the toppings are always according to your personal preferences.
8. Your dish is ready to be served.

5.5 Black Bean Tacos

Cooking Time: 45 minutes

Serving Size: 4

Ingredients:
- Smoked paprika, one tbsp.
- Salt and pepper to taste
- Corn tortillas, eight
- Cilantro, two tbsp.
- Cumin, one tsp.
- Black beans, half cup
- Mushrooms, one cup
- Red bell pepper, one
- Olive oil, one tbsp.
- Avocado slices, as required
- Salsa, as required
- Jalapeno slices, half cup
- Monetary Jack cheese, half cup
- Avocado cream, one cup

Instructions:
1. Cook the black beans, add the spices, mushrooms and cook for thirty minutes until the beans are done.
2. Arrange the cooked mixture on the tortillas.

3. Add the cheese on it and bake it for five minutes.
4. Add the avocado cream on top of it.
5. Place jalapeno slices, avocado slices and salsa on top.
6. You can change the toppings if you want.
7. Garnish it with fresh cilantro leaves.
8. Your dish is ready to be served.

5.6 Kidney Bean Fajita Tacos

Cooking Time: 45 minutes

Serving Size:

Ingredients:

- Smoked paprika, one tbsp.
- Salt and pepper to taste
- Corn tortillas, eight
- Cilantro, two tbsp.
- Cumin, one tsp.
- Kidney beans, half cup
- Red bell pepper, one
- Green bell pepper, one
- Red bell pepper, one
- Olive oil, one tbsp.
- Avocado slices, as required
- Salsa, as required
- Jalapeno slices, half cup
- Monetary Jack cheese, half cup

- Avocado cream, one cup

Instructions:

1. Cook the kidney beans, add the spices, red bell pepper, green bell pepper, and cook for thirty minutes until the beans are done.
2. Arrange the cooked mixture on the tortillas.
3. Add the cheese on it and bake it for five minutes.
4. Add the avocado cream on top of it.
5. Place jalapeno slices, avocado slices and salsa on top.
6. You can change the toppings if you want.
7. Garnish it with fresh cilantro leaves.
8. Your dish is ready to be served.

5.7 Cauliflower Walnut Taco

Cooking Time: 15 minutes

Serving Size: 4

Ingredients:

- Cauliflower, two cups
- Paprika, one tsp.
- Cumin powder, one tsp.
- Oregano, one tsp.
- Salt and pepper, as required
- Chili flakes, one tsp.
- Olive oil, two tbsp.
- Salsa, half cup
- Cilantro, as required

- Taco shells, four
- Walnut, one cup
- Sour cream, as required
- Creamy cilantro sauce, as required

Instructions:
1. Roast the cauliflower by adding all the spices and olive oil.
2. Roast for ten minutes.
3. Add the cauliflower in the taco shells; add salsa, sour cream, creamy cilantro sauce, and cilantro on top.
4. Add the crushed walnuts on top.
5. Your dish is ready to be served.

5.8 Tofu Tacos

Cooking Time: 15 minutes

Serving Size: 4

Ingredients:
- Tofu, two cups
- Paprika, one tsp.
- Cumin powder, one tsp.
- Oregano, one tsp.
- Salt and pepper, as required
- Chili flakes, one tsp.
- Olive oil, two tbsp.
- Salsa, half cup
- Cilantro, as required

- Taco shells, four
- Sour cream, as required
- Creamy cilantro sauce, as required

Instructions:
1. Roast the tofu squares by adding all the spices and olive oil.
2. Roast for ten minutes.
3. Add the tofu mixture in the taco shells; add salsa, sour cream, creamy cilantro sauce, and cilantro on top.
4. Your dish is ready to be served.

5.9 Quorn Chili Taco

Cooking Time: 20 minutes

Serving Size: 6

Ingredients:
- Olive oil, two tbsp.
- Tomatoes, one cup
- Shallots, half cup
- Mix spice, two tbsp.
- Chili, one
- Garlic, one
- Taco shells, eight
- Sweetcorn, one cup
- Water, two tbsp.
- Quorn mince, two cups

Instructions:

1. Add the olive oil to a saucepan and heat over a medium heat.
2. Sauté the garlic, shallots, chili, and red pepper.
3. Add the Quorn mince, using a wooden spoon, break up the mince.
4. Sprinkle in the spices and the whole rehydrated chili.
5. Cook for five minutes.
6. Add the chopped tomatoes, sweetcorn, and water.
7. Leave to cook over a low-medium heat for ten minutes, until all of the ingredients are cooked through.
8. Add the mixture on to the preheated taco shells.
9. Add your preferred toppings.
10. Your dish is ready to be served.

5.10 Vegan Birria Tacos

Cooking Time: 25 minutes

Serving Size: 4

Ingredients:

- Mushrooms, one cup
- Dried chilies, three
- Onion, one cup
- Garlic, one
- Creamy red sauce, as required
- Salt and pepper to taste
- Olive oil, two tbsp.

- Mix cheese, one cup
- Cilantro, as required
- Taco shells, eight
- Taco seasoning mix, one tsp.

Instructions:
1. Cook the mushrooms in the olive oil.
2. Add onions into it and cook until soft and translucent.
3. Next, add the garlic, and dried chilies into the mixture.
4. Add the taco seasoning into the mixture and cook for five minutes.
5. Heat the taco shells in an oven.
6. Fill the taco sheets with the above mixture.
7. Add the creamy red sauce, and cilantro leaves on top.
8. Your dish is ready to be served.

5.11 Tacos Al Pastor

Cooking Time: 30 minutes

Serving Size: 4

Ingredients:
- Chili powder, one tsp.
- Pork shoulder, one pound
- Mix spice, one tbsp.
- Pineapple, one cup
- Salt and pepper to taste
- Olive oil, two tbsp.
- Avocado, one

- Cilantro, as required
- Tortilla sheets, eight
- Pineapple juice, half cup

Instructions:
1. Marinate the pork shoulder and pineapple chunks in the spice mix, chili powder, olive oil, salt and pepper.
2. Grill the pork shoulder for twenty minutes.
3. Then slice the pineapple chunks and pork shoulder into pieces.
4. Lightly heat the tortilla sheet and place the meat and pineapple on the tortilla.
5. Add the avocado slices, and fresh cilantro leaves.
6. Roll the tortillas.
7. Your dish is ready to be served.

5.12 Tex- Mex Vegetarian Tacos

Cooking Time: 15 minutes

Serving Size: 8

Ingredients:
- Jalapeño, one to two
- Tomatoes, two
- Green bell pepper, one
- Red potatoes, two to three
- Freshly chopped parsley and cilantro, two tbsp.
- Salt and pepper to taste
- Onion, half

- Tortillas, eight
- Shredded cheese, half cup
- Red bell pepper, one
- Sour cream, as required
- Cilantro creamy sauce, as required

Instructions:

1. Add a little olive oil in the pan.
2. Cut the tomatoes, jalapenos, onions, and cilantro.
3. Cook the red bell pepper, green bell pepper, peas, and red onion.
4. Chop the potatoes into small cubes and cook with a little bit of olive oil, garlic, salt and pepper until they are slightly crispy.
5. Heat the tortilla in a frying pan and add the shredded cheese.
6. Combine the potatoes, and mix vegetables.
7. Add the ingredients on the tortillas.
8. Top with sour cream, and cilantro creamy sauce.
9. Serve your dish with fresh salsa.

5.13 Jackfruit Tacos

Cooking Time: 25 minutes

Serving Size: 8

Ingredients:

- Jackfruit, two cups
- Onion, one
- Vegetable broth, half cup

- Chili powder, one tsp.
- Smoked paprika, one tsp.
- Agave, one tbsp.
- Taco shells, eight
- Avocado, one
- Cilantro, a bunch

Instructions:
1. Cook the jackfruit chunks in vegetable oil.
2. Add agave, onions, chili powder, smoked paprika powder, and vegetable broth in it.
3. Cook the mixture for ten minutes.
4. Heat the taco shells in an oven for a few minutes.
5. Add the above cooked mixture into it.
6. Next, add your preferred toppings.
7. Add avocado and cilantro on top.
8. Your meal is ready to be served.

5.14 Zucchini and Crimini Tacos

Cooking Time: 20 minutes

Serving Size: 4

Ingredients:
- Pico de Galo, one cup
- Mix spice, one tbsp.
- Crimini, one cup
- Salt and pepper to taste
- Olive oil, two tbsp.

- Zucchini, one cup
- Cilantro, as required
- Taco shells, eight
- Creamy cilantro sauce, as required
- Onion, one
- Garlic, one

Instructions:
1. In the olive oil, add the onions.
2. Cook the onions until soft.
3. Add the Cremini crushed garlic.
4. Cook for two minutes and then add crimini and zucchini.
5. Add the mix spice, salt and pepper.
6. Lightly heat the taco shells.
7. Now add the above mixture into the taco shells.
8. Add the creamy cilantro sauce and pico de gallo on top.
9. Garnish with fresh cilantro leaves.
10. Your dish is ready to be served.

5.15 Potato Tacos

Cooking Time: 20 minutes

Serving Size: 4

Ingredients:
- Fresh salsa, one cup
- Mix spice, one tbsp.
- Cooked potatoes, one cup

- Salt and pepper to taste
- Olive oil, two tbsp.
- Refried beans, one cup
- Cilantro, as required
- Taco shells, eight
- Creamy red sauce, one tbsp.
- Taco seasoning, one tsp.
- Red onions, one

Instructions:
1. Add the olive oil in a pan.
2. Add the cooked potatoes and refried beans into it.
3. Add the mix spices, taco seasoning, salt and pepper.
4. Cook for five minutes.
5. Next, heat the taco shells in an oven for a few minutes.
6. Add the above made mixture into the taco shells.
7. Top with creamy red sauce and cilantro.
8. Add the red onion slices.
9. Your dish is ready to be served.

5.16 Vegetarian Taco Lasagna

Cooking Time: 15 minutes

Serving Size: 4

Ingredients:
- Pico de Galo, one cup
- Mix vegetable, one cup

- Shredded chicken, one cup
- Salt and pepper to taste
- Olive oil, two tbsp.
- Mix cheese, one cup
- Refried beans, one cup
- Cilantro, as required
- Tortilla sheets, eight

Instructions:

1. Add the mix vegetables in a pan and cook for few minutes.
2. Add all the spices and refried beans.
3. Add salt and pepper.
4. Once cooked add the mixture into the tortillas.
5. Add Pico de Galo on top.
6. Roll and place it in a baking tray.
7. Add cheese on top and bake.
8. Bake for five minutes until cheese is melted.
9. Add some fresh cilantro leaves on top.
10. Your dish is ready to be served.

5.17 Mushroom Tacos

Cooking Time: 15 minutes

Serving Size: 4

Ingredients:

- Pico de Galo, one cup
- Mix cheese, one cup

- Shredded mushrooms, one cup
- Salt and pepper to taste
- Olive oil, two tbsp.
- Cilantro, as required
- Tortilla sheets, eight
- Sour cream, as required

Instructions:
1. Add the mushrooms in the olive oil.
2. Add salt and pepper into the mushrooms.
3. Lightly heat the tortilla sheets.
4. Add the cooked mushrooms on top of the tortillas.
5. Add the pico de gallo on top.
6. Add the sour cream on top.
7. Garnish it with cilantro leaves.
8. Your dish is ready to be served.

5.18 Chickpea and Cauliflower Tacos

Cooking Time: 20 minutes

Serving Size: 4

Ingredients:
- Pico de Galo, one cup
- Mix spice, two tbsp.
- Cooked chickpeas, one cup
- Salt and pepper to taste
- Olive oil, two tbsp.

- Roasted cauliflower, one cup
- Cilantro, as required
- Tortilla sheets, eight
- Taco seasoning, one tap.
- Sour cream, as required
- Creamy cilantro sauce, as required

Instructions:
1. Add the chickpeas in the olive oil.
2. Add the roasted cauliflower on top.
3. Add the mix spice, salt, taco seasoning, and pepper.
4. Lightly fry the tortillas.
5. Add the above mixture on top, add the sour cream, and creamy cilantro sauce on top.
6. Garnish it with fresh cilantro leaves.
7. Your dish is ready to be served.

5.19 Pumpkin Tacos

Cooking Time: 25 minutes

Serving Size: 4

Ingredients:
- Fresh salsa, one cup
- Mix spice, one tsp.
- Pumpkin cubes, one cup
- Salt and pepper to taste
- Olive oil, two tbsp.
- Sour cream, as required

- Cilantro, as required
- Tortilla sheets, eight

Instructions:
1. Add the pumpkin cubes in the olive oil.
2. Add the mix spice, salt, and pepper in it.
3. Lightly fry the tortillas.
4. Add the mixture above on the tortillas.
5. Add the fresh salsa, sour cream on top.
6. Garnish it with freshly chopped cilantro leaves.
7. Your dish is ready to be served.

5.20 Mexican Zucchini Tacos

Cooking Time: 15 minutes

Serving Size: 4

Ingredients:
- Pico de Galo, one cup
- Mexican mix spice, one tbsp.
- Shredded zucchini, one cup
- Salt and pepper to taste
- Olive oil, two tbsp.
- Taco seasoning, one tsp.
- Cilantro, as required
- Taco shells, eight
- Tomatoes, one cup
- Sour cream, as required

Instructions:
1. Add the zucchini in the olive oil.
2. Add the salt, pepper, Mexican spice mix, and tomatoes.
3. Cook properly for ten minutes.
4. Heat the taco shells for five minutes.
5. Add the mixture in the taco shells.
6. Add Pico de Galo on top.
7. Add the sour cream and cilantro leaves on top.
8. Your dish is ready to be served.

The above recipes are easy to make, delicious, and nutritious at the same time. So, start cooking your yummy Mexican taco meals at home.

Conclusion

Mexican cuisine is extremely versatile and diverse cuisine. It originated from Mexico but has spread worldwide and it is presently loved and eaten everywhere in the world. The people of the United Stated of America love Mexican food and they consume it on daily basis.

The reason behind the high popularity of the Mexican food is due to the recent fashion of street food. Street style food items are loved all over the world. Mexican food contains the ever-famous street food me the tacos that are consumed in a very high ratio in America. In this book, we have given seventy-seven different recipes of tacos that comprise of diverse dishes that you would love to consume.

The recipes include healthy breakfast, lunch, dinner, snacks, and vegetarian recipes. A person who does not usually cook, can easily make all these recipes with the detailed ingredient list and easy to follow instructions that are mentioned with each recipe in the book. After reading this book, you will be able to make your food all by your own without the need of going out to get your favorite tacos.

Vegetarian Mexican Cookbook

77 Recipes for Homemade Vegetarian Mexican Dishes.

By

Adele Tyler

© **Copyright 2020 by Adele Tyler - All rights reserved.**

This document is geared towards providing exact and reliable information in regard to the topic and issue covered. The publication is sold with the idea that the publisher is not required to render accounting, officially permitted, or otherwise, qualified services. If advice is necessary, legal or professional, a practiced individual in the profession should be ordered.

From a Declaration of Principles which was accepted and approved equally by a Committee of the American Bar Association and a Committee of Publishers and Associations.

In no way is it legal to reproduce, duplicate, or transmit any part of this document in either electronic means or in printed format. Recording of this publication is strictly prohibited and any storage of this document is not allowed unless with written permission from the publisher. All rights reserved.

The information provided herein is stated to be truthful and consistent, in that any liability, in terms of inattention or otherwise, by any usage or abuse of any policies, processes, or directions contained within is the solitary and utter responsibility of the recipient reader. Under no circumstances will any legal responsibility or blame be held against the publisher for any reparation, damages, or monetary loss due to the information herein, either directly or indirectly.

Respective authors own all copyrights not held by the publisher.

The information herein is offered for informational purposes solely and is universal as so. The presentation of the information is without contract or any type of guarantee assurance.

The trademarks that are used are without any consent, and the publication of the trademark is without permission or backing by the trademark owner.

All trademarks and brands within this book are for clarifying purposes only and are owned by the owners themselves, not affiliated with this document.

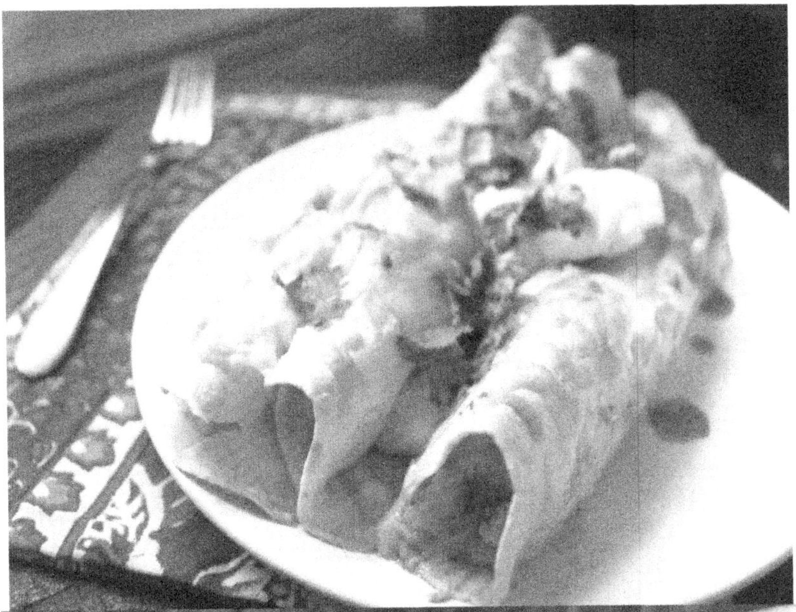

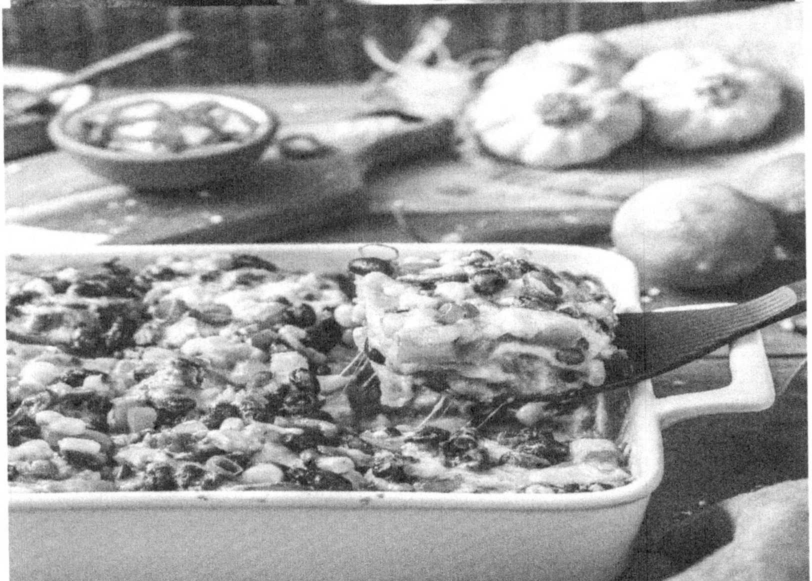

Table of Contents

INTRODUCTION 8

CHAPTER 01: VEGETARIAN MEXICAN BREAKFAST RECIPES 11

CHAPTER 02: VEGETARIAN MEXICAN LUNCH RECIPES 35

CHAPTER 03: VEGETARIAN MEXICAN SNACKS RECIPES 60

CHAPTER 04: VEGETARIAN MEXICAN DINNER RECIPES 88

CONCLUSION..110

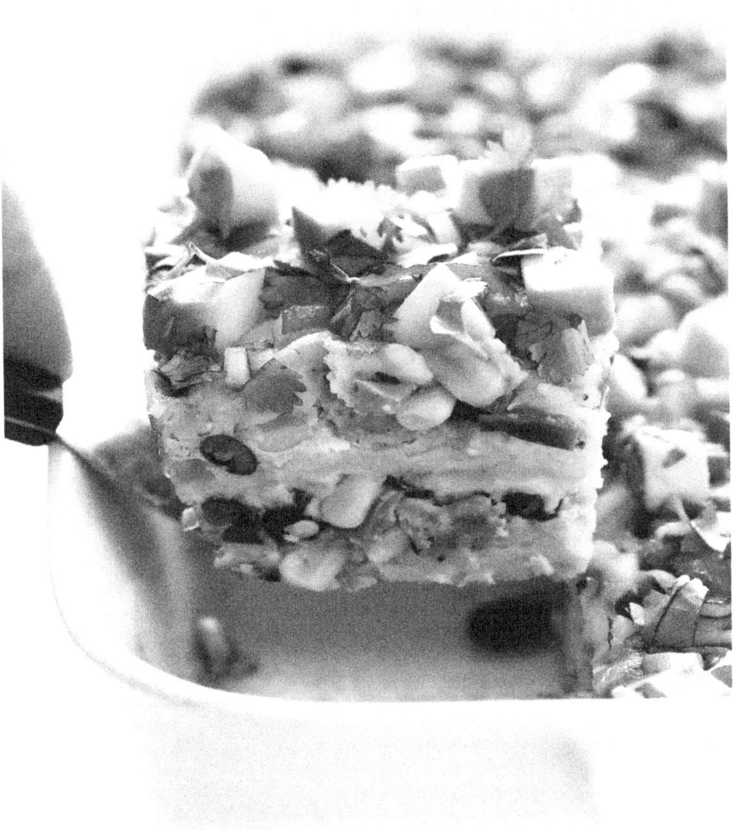

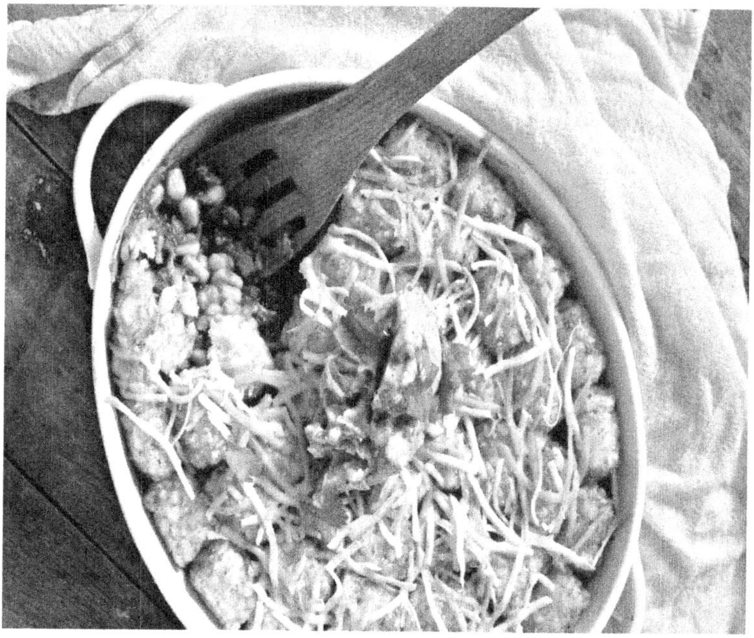

Introduction

Mexico is more stunning than the pure blue seas and tropical culture. Mexican food is famous for being delicious and exclusive. There is so much more to be found than burritos, chips, and guacamole in the Mexican food. You will note how essential and special cuisine is as you turn your attention through Mexico. All are entirely natural and delicious, abundant in color and taste, complete with seasonings that have a fair impact.

There is a lively background of authentic Mexican cuisine, and it is connected to the center of Mexican culture and ideals. To learn the Mexican roots, one of the best approaches is to learn its cuisine. Three major Mexican civilizations derive from many of the tastes, sights and sounds of traditional Mexican cuisine: Mayan, Aztec, and Spain.

The Mayans were nomadic, and the Mayan civilization is host to some of the most common foods. A staple was food made from maize, which is where corn tortillas are created. The Aztec Kingdom was in full force by the 1300s. Through their way of existence, the Aztecs would incorporate salt, pepper, and even cocoa. Spain conquered Mexico two hundred years later, and Mexican society was exposed to a whole bunch of modern foods. They imported dairy goods, cloves, and several spices and herbs.

The food system of Mexico is strongly rooted in meat-eating. They usually speak of beef tacos and meat dishes when people speak about Mexican cuisine. Although most Mexicans may have chuckled at people who do not consume meat a few years earlier but the vegetarian diet has now been embraced and incorporated into the cuisine of Mexico. Being so near to the United States, patterns, from entertainment to clothes, are inspired by American society, and food is no different. Now, residents of Mexico are also accepting a vegan diet.

The vegetarian aspect of Mexico is, however, less stated, but just as popular. Mexico is all about citrus fruits, legume forms, a wide variety of herbs, and a preference of fresh ingredients for cooking. It is a meat-focused nation, and there is no common vegetarianism, but thankfully in many dishes, there are vegetarian ingredients such as corn tortillas, rice, cheese, and vegetables.

In Mexico, the strongest choices for vegetarians are Enchilada, Quesadilla, Burritos, Meatless Lasagna, Pies, Vegan tacos, Tortillas and many more. These quick and inexpensive snacks can be found at street stalls. Most of these are focused on corn tortillas, and even if it is just cheese, you can normally get vegetarian variants and then liven them up with traditional toppings such as salsas. In this chapter, you will come to know about Vegetarian Mexican breakfast, lunch, snacks and dinner recipes.

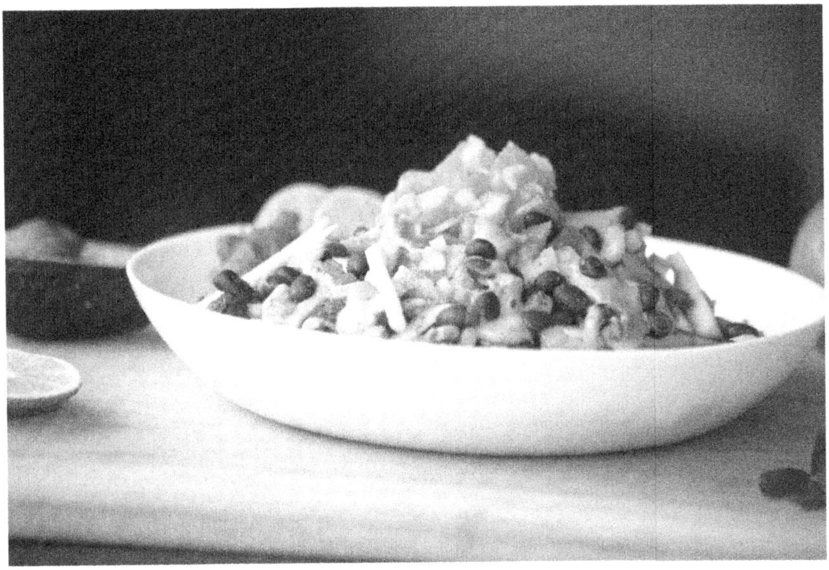

Chapter 01: Vegetarian Mexican Breakfast Recipes

Flavorful breakfasts are common in Mexico. They are the start of your day. If you eat healthy and fresh at the beginning of your day, it is guaranteed that you would feel the same throughout the course of the day. Recipes in this chapter are for vegetarian persons.

❖ **Chorizo and Eggs Ranchero**

Time to cook: 25 minutes

Servings: 2

Ingredients:
- Tortillas (2 piece)
- Oil for frying
- ½ cup of beans (refried)
- ½ cup of chorizo
- 4 eggs (beaten)
- Half cup of salsa (medium)
- Half cup of cheese (shredded)

Instructions:
1. Firstly, set the oven to 425 degrees and let it warm. Moisturize the tortillas on both edges with oil. Bake for 12 minutes or until the surfaces turn brown. Let it cool for 5 minutes.
2. Roast the beans in the oven for 3-5 minutes.
3. Cook and scramble chorizo over a moderate flame in a broad skillet for 4-6 minutes or until it is cooked properly.
4. Clean the pan. Include eggs in it and scramble it. Fry it until browned. Heat salsa in the oven.
5. Assemble all the products over tortillas and serve it with cheese.

❖ Sopaipillas

Time to cook: 35 minutes

Servings: 12

Ingredients:
- 1 cup flour (all purpose)
- ½ teaspoon of baking powder
- Salt as per your taste
- ½ cup of warm water
- Oil
- ½ teaspoon of honey

Instructions:
1. Mix the rice, baking powder and salt in a wide dish. Tighten the paste until it resembles fine crumbs. Add water slowly and mix it properly.
2. Knead the dough for 2 minutes on a floured place. Cover and set it aside for 10 minutes.
3. Put the dough in the rectangle shape. Carve into 12 squares with a cutter.
4. Heat deep-oil fryer. Fry the sopaipillas on either hand for 1-2 minutes.
5. Drain on towels made of paper; stay wet. Serving with honey if needed

❖ Mexican Pancakes

Servings: 10

Time taken: 25 minutes

Ingredients:

- 2 cups of flour
- 1 cup of sugar and cinnamon
- Three Eggs (beaten)
- ½ cup of buttermilk
- ½ cup of sugar (powder)
- Ice-cream vanilla or honey for serving

Instructions:

1. In a cup, merge flour with sugar and mix them together. Eggs, milk and butter are whisked together.
2. Heat a skillet over moderate heat and cook a half cup of mixture for 3 minutes from both sides or until bubbles emerge on the top.
3. Serve with vanilla ice cream.

❖ **Huevos Rancheros**

Total time: 20 minutes

Servings: 4

Ingredients:
- Vegetable oil
- 4 tortillas (maize)
- 1 cup of beans (fried)
- One tablespoon of butter
- 4 eggs
- 1 cup of cheese (shredded)

- Half cup of salsa for serving

Instructions:
1. Melt butter over a moderate flame in a shallow skillet. Fry the tortillas for three minutes. Flush the grease from it by using paper towels.
2. In an oven, mix the refried beans and butter. Cook them in the oven until fully warmed. When the tortillas are cooked, fry in the skillet over simple eggs.
3. On the bowls, put the tortillas and spread a layer of beans on them.
4. Garnish with cheese, egg and salsa.

❖ **Loaded Vegetables and Chorizo Egg Casserole**

Time taken: 20 minutes

Servings: 4

Ingredients:
- Olive oil
- One onion (chopped)
- One cup of peas
- One potato (finely diced)
- Two chorizos (chopped)
- Two bell peppers (chopped)
- 1 cup of kale

- Salt and pepper as per your taste
- One tomato (chopped)
- 5 eggs
- Thyme and paprika
- 2 cups of cheese (shredded)
- Half cup of parmesan (shredded)

Instructions:

1. Warm the oil in a pan over a moderate flame. Add the onion and mushrooms and simmer until the mushrooms start browning.
2. Insert other vegetables, chorizo and spices in it and let them cook for around 10 minutes, stirring sometimes.
3. Place the vegetables in a 9-11 inch casserole dish and mix the tomatoes in it.
4. Mix the eggs with the paprika, cheese and thyme in a cup thoroughly.
5. In the casserole bowl, spill the eggs over the vegetables and blend until everything is well mixed.
6. Cover the casserole dish with anything and store it for one day at least.
7. Preheat the oven up to 270C and put the casserole in it and let it bake for 30 minutes. Serve it.

❖ **Chiles Rellenos Soufflé**

Time taken: 35 minutes

Servings: 6

Ingredients:
- Two cans of green chiles (cooked)
- 1 cup of cheese (sliced)
- 2 bell peppers (chopped)
- Four eggs
- ½ cup of milk
- Salt and pepper as per your taste
- Cilantro sprigs for serving

Instructions:
1. Preheat the oven to 220C. Sprinkle the oil over baking dish and place the chiles with slices of cheese in it. Sprinkle it with spices.
2. Mix the egg yolks and milk in a small bowl with a blender until it is well mixed. Also, add flour and salt to stir until smooth.
3. Whisk the egg whites in a wide bowl with the blender. Fold the yolk mixture softly into this. Mix the spoon uniformly over the stuffed chiles.
4. Bake for 35 minutes. Garnish with cilantro sprigs for each serving.

❖ **Green Chile Quiche Squares**

Time taken: 35 minutes

Servings: 3

Ingredients:
- 4 eggs
- Salt and pepper as per your taste
- One tablespoon sauce with cayenne pepper
- 3 cans of green chiles (diced)
- 2 cups of cheese (grated)
- 1 cup of cheddar cheese (shredded)

Instructions:
1. Firstly, preheated the oven up to 250C.
2. Grease the baking dish.
3. Add all ingredients in a cup. Blend well together.
4. In the baking dish, push the mixture down and bake for 40 minutes or until the center is firm
5. Enable to cool, then slice and serve in tiny squares.

❖ **Vegetable Omelet Cups**

Servings: 4

Total Time: 50 Minutes

Ingredients:
- ½ cup of tomatoes
- ½ cup of water

- Three eggs
- 1 tablespoon of coriander (minced)
- Butter (melted)
- Salt and pepper as per your taste
- 1 cup of cheese (shredded)
- One onion (chopped)
- Olive oil
- 2 tablespoons of olives (diced)

Instructions:
1. Combine the eggs, egg whites, cilantro, sugar, salt, pepper and water in a big cup.
2. Place a pan over moderate flame and sprinkle oil in it. Heat it for 2 minutes. Dump into the middle of the skillet around a half cup of the egg mixture — Cook for 3 minutes. Then, change the side and cook for 1 minute.
3. Remove and put it in a baking dish covered with cooking spray. Repeat with the remaining egg mixture and produce three more cups of an omelet.
4. Sprinkle cheese over it.
5. Preheat the oven to 350 degrees.
6. Simmer all chopped vegetables in the oil in a separate pan over a moderate flame until it turns soft. Spoon into cups of omelets.
7. Sprinkle the cheese over it.
8. Bake for 10-12 minutes or until it turns brown. Serve it warm.

❖ Flapjack

Time taken: 30 minutes

Servings: 3

Ingredients:
- Butter
- Brown Sugar
- Oats of porridge
- Golden syrup

Instructions:
1. Firstly, preheat the oven up to 180C.
2. Place a pan over a moderate flame. Put the butter, sugar, oats and syrup in it. Sauté it for 5 minutes.
3. Grease a baking dish with cooking oil.
4. Shift the flapjack mixture to the baking pan with oil.
5. Put for 30 minutes in the preheated oven or until the sides tend to turn brown.
6. Cut them into slices and serve.

❖ Cheese Enchiladas

Time: 35 minutes

Servings: 5

Ingredients:
- 1 cup of cheddar cheese (shredded)
- 5 tortillas (maize)
- Oil
- One onion (chopped)
- Enchilada salsa (cooked)
- Guacamole
- Sour milk

Instructions:
1. Firstly, preheat the oven up to 250C. Fry tortillas in the frying oil in a separate pan.
2. Soak the tortillas in spicy enchilada sauce to coat them after you do this. Now, place the tortillas on a plate for a minute to cool off.
3. Put grated cheese over it then sprinkle the middle of one tortilla with some onion and fold it.
4. Lightly bake it in the oven.
5. Serve it.

❖ Mexican Filed Omelet

Servings: 8

Time needed: 40 minutes

Ingredients:
- One avocado
- Three limes
- Cilantro
- Yoghurt
- Olive oil
- One onion (chopped)
- 1 carrot (chopped)
- Salt and pepper as per your taste
- Eight eggs
- 1 cup of cheese (shredded)

Instructions:
1. In a mixer, squeeze the avocado flesh. Rip the cilantro stalks, apply the yoghurt and a splash of oil and blend it well. Add seasoning and lime in it.
2. Chop all the other ingredients.
3. Mix vegetables, blended mixture, cheese and eggs together.
4. Put oil in the pan over a moderate heat. Add quarter of egg mixture in it. Gently cook the omelet for 3 minutes.
5. Serve it.

❖ **Mexican Style Sandwich**

Time taken: 25 minutes

Servings: 2

Ingredients:
- Four white bread slices
- Half cup of beans (refried)
- Four tablespoons of corn (cooked)
- Cheese (shredded)
- Two chili peppers (chopped)

Instructions:
1. Place a sheet of refried beans over each piece of bread.
2. Assemble all other ingredients over that layer.
3. In a sandwich maker, grill the sandwiches for 5 minutes or until the cheese starts to melt.

❖ **Apple Pie Baked French Toast**

Servings: 10

Time to cook: 50 minutes

Ingredients:
- 20 pieces of bread
- Apple pie sauce
- Eight Eggs (beaten)
- 2 cups of milk
- Vanilla extract (1 teaspoon)
- Cinnamon (1 teaspoon)

For Topping:
- Half cup of brown sugar
- Half cup of butter

Instructions:
1. Assemble ten bread slices in a greased baking dish. Spread over the filling of the pie.
2. Mix all other ingredients thoroughly. Pour over the bread.
3. Bake for 35-40 minutes in a preheated oven up to 250C.
4. Serve it.

❖ **Spinach and Mushroom Egg Muffins**

Servings: 6

Time taken: 35 minutes

Ingredients:

- Six Eggs
- Half cup of milk
- One teaspoon of garlic (powdered)
- Salt and pepper as per your taste
- 2 cups of spinach (chopped)
- 6 ounce of mushrooms (diced)

Instructions:

1. Firstly, preheat the furnace to 350F.
2. Add the eggs, cream and all seasonings to a wide mixing dish. Properly whisk together.
3. Cut the mushrooms and spinach and whisk them into the mixture.
4. Put a full spoon of this mixture in a greased muffin tins.
5. Bake it all for 30 minutes. Serve it.

❖ Fried Egg Toast

Servings: 4

Period Required: 25 minutes

Ingredients:

- Four sandwich bread slices
- Olive oil
- Four eggs
- 1 tomato (chopped)
- Spices as per your taste
- 2 cups of parmesan cheese (shredded)

Instructions:

1. Make a void in the middle of each bread slice using a cutter. Warm oil over moderate to high heat in a skillet. Cook for approximately 2 minutes.
2. Place a mixture of eggs and other ingredients in that void. Decrease the heat to low. Put a lid over a skillet and cook for 3 to 4 minutes.
3. Serve it.

❖ **Aztec Baked Eggs**

Servings: 6

Time taken: 35 minutes

Ingredients:
- Butter
- Six Eggs
- Pepper and salt, to taste
- Other ingredients include chopped ham, chopped green onions and shredded cheese.

Instructions:
1. Firstly, preheat the furnace to 250C.
2. Grease muffin tins with oil.

3. Put one egg in each muffin tin. Insert ingredients of your choosing.
4. Bake for 13 minutes. Immediately serve.

❖ **Eggs with Fried Tortillas**

Servings: 2

Period required: 30 minutes

Ingredients:
- Two eggs
- 2 tortillas
- One onion and tomato (chopped)
- Coriander
- Olive oil as per your need
- Salt and pepper as per your taste

Instructions:
1. In a skillet, heat the oil, insert chopped vegetables and sauté for around 5 minutes or until tender.
2. Add all the spices in it and let it simmer for 2 minutes.
3. Put the beaten eggs into the pan and cook for 4-5 minutes over a mild fire, stirring until the eggs are lightly scrambled.

4. Warm the tortillas. Split the tortillas between the eggs and serve.

❖ Mexican Style Corn

Total time: 35 minutes

Servings: 4

Ingredients:
- Four ears of corn
- ½ cup of mayonnaise
- ½ cup of parmesan cheese (shredded)
- Chili, pepper and salt as per your taste

Instructions:
1. Boil ears of corn in a pan filled with water over moderate heat for 25 minutes or until it turn soft.
2. Pour mayonnaise all over the kernels. Sprinkle the Parmesan cheese evenly around the ear and chili powder.
3. Repeat with the leftover corn ears.

❖ Churro Doughnuts

Servings: 12

Time taken: 45 minutes

Ingredients:
- Half cup of sugar (melted)
- 1 teaspoon of vanilla essence
- Three Eggs
- Salt (pinch)
- Cinnamon (half teaspoon)
- 2 cups of flour
- One teaspoon of baking powder
- One cup of milk

Instructions:

1. Whisk in the butter until foamy. Add sugar and vanilla extract steadily and beat them to produce a smooth mixture.
2. Combine the baking powder and the rice, cinnamon and nutmeg. To the creamed mixture, apply the flour mixture alternately with the milk.
3. Spoon the doughnut batter into a non-stick baking tin. Put in the 350 F preheated oven and bake for 15 minutes or until the toothpick inserted into the doughnut comes out clean.
4. Garnish it with any topping.

❖ Sweet Potato Hash

Serving: 1

Period Required: 40 minutes.

Ingredients:
- One sweet potato (diced)
- Olive oil
- 1 onion (diced)
- 1 teaspoon of cumin
- Chili powder, salt and pepper as per your need
- ½ teaspoon of garlic
- One egg
- 3 tablespoons of mozzarella cheese (shredded)

Instructions:
1. Cook your finely sliced sweet potato for about 10-15 minutes.
2. In a pan, heat up the olive oil and add your onions, red pepper, sweet potato and spices in it.
3. Keep frying until the exterior of the sweet potato becomes crispy.
4. Spread it all in the pan equally and smash an egg in the middle. Cook until the egg white is almost cooked.
5. Sprinkle shredded mozzarella over it and put under the skillet until it is melted.

6. Serve it with anything.

Chapter 02: Vegetarian Mexican Lunch Recipes

The main meals of a day are usually taken for lunch. We typically have light breakfast and dinner but have a heavy lunch. A list of such recipes has been shared in this chapter which can be served for lunch. These lunch recipes are specifically Vegetarian Mexican Lunch recipes. Let us just dig into it.

❖ **Mexican Black Beans and Rice**

Servings: 4

Time took: 35 minutes

Ingredients:
- Oil as per you required
- One small onion (chopped)
- Clove of garlic (minced)
- ½ tablespoon of cumin
- 1 tablespoon of tomato (puree)
- Water
- Salt and pepper as per your taste
- Grain rice (250g)
- One tablespoon of coriander
- Beans (rinsed and washed)

Instructions:
1. Preheat oil in a pan over moderate flame. For 5 minutes, sauté the onion and garlic or until it turns tender.
2. Add all other ingredients, spices and the rice in it and let it cook for 10 minutes. Put a lid over a pan and lower the temperature and cook it until the rice is tender and the water has been diluted.

3. Add black beans in it and let it cook until it is fully cooked.
4. Serve it.

❖ Black Bean Lasagna

Servings: 10

Time required: 35 minutes

Ingredients:
- One onion (chopped)
- One green pepper (chopped)
- Oil
- 4 to 6 cloves of garlic (minced)
- 1 can of tomato (puree)
- Salt, pepper and chili as per your taste
- One can black beans (rinsed)
- 1 cup of pinto beans (rinsed)
- Three cups of cheese (shredded)
- One egg (beaten)
- Parsley
- Four tortillas (halved)

Instructions:

1. Put a pan with oil over a moderate flame. Add onion, garlic, tomatoes and spices in it and let it simmer for 5-8 minutes.
2. Add beans in it and let it cook for another 10 minutes.
3. Grease a baking a dish. Put half of the mixture of bean in it. Spread it thoroughly over it.
4. Mix cheese, egg white and jalapeno in the separate bowl and put this mixture in a baking dish. Make layers like this.
5. Bake in a preheated oven at 350C for 25 minutes.
6. Let it cool first, then serve it.

❖ **Jicama Tortillas**

Servings: 4

Period required: 15 minutes

Ingredients:

- One medium Jicama
- Olive Oil
- Salt and pepper as per your need
- Paprika

Instructions:
1. Firstly, peel and slice jicama into tortillas.
2. Drizzle oil, salt and paprika over it.
3. Heat the tortillas on either side for about a minute, before they are soft and slightly tender.
4. Serve them with anything of your liking.

❖ **Black Bean & Quinoa Enchilada**

Servings: 5

Total time: 30 minutes

Ingredients:
- 1 cup of quinoa (rinsed and washed)
- One tin of black beans (rinsed and washed)
- One sweet potato (peeled and sliced)
- 2 cups of maize
- 1 cup of tomatoes (diced)
- Taco seasoning
- One cup of enchilada sauce
- Water

- 2 cups of spinach (chopped)
- ½ cup of Mexican cheese blend

Instructions:
1. Mix the cleaned all ingredients, spices and 1/2 cup of water in a moderate pan.
2. Put a lid over it and let it cook until the quinoa turns soft.
3. Simmer in the cheese and spinach.
4. Serve it with any of topping.

❖ **Caramelized Onion & Jalapeno Quesadilla**

Time required: 35 minutes.

Servings: 10

Ingredients:
- Olive oil
- One big onion (chopped)
- 1 tablespoon of balsamic vinegar
- One teaspoon of sugar
- Ten tortillas
- 1 cup of fontina cheese (shredded)
- 1 cup of goat cheese (shredded)

Instructions:

1. Firstly you have to caramelized onion for this, heat olive oil and onions in a pan. Cook until it turns soft.
2. Add spices and sugar in it and let it simmer for 4 minutes.
3. Grease a baking dish and place three tortillas and put cheese and caramelized onions over it. Cover it with tortillas. Brush the top of tortillas with olive oil.
4. Put the dish in a preheated oven at 250C for 10 minutes or until the tortillas turn brown.
5. Serve it.

- ❖ **Santa Fe Veggie Quesadilla**

Servings: 4

Period Required: 10 minutes

Ingredients:

- 1 tortilla
- 1 cup of cheese (shredded)
- Half cup of corn (drained)
- Half cup of red bell pepper (chopped)
- Half cup of black beans (rinsed and washed)
- One onion (chopped)

Instructions:

1. Over moderate flame, cook a finely oiled medium pan. To provide an equal layer of oil on all sides, put the tortilla in the pan and turn it again.
2. Enable 3 minutes to heat the tortilla on the one hand.
3. Layer the cheese mixture uniformly, starting at the middle of the tortilla, until the whole layer of the tortilla is coated. Place the vegetables on top of the cheese.
4. Cut tortilla and serve it warm.

❖ **Bean Burrito**

Servings: 8

Time required: 60 minutes

Ingredients:

- 1 cup of rice
- Olive oil
- Two onions (chopped)
- Four cloves of garlic (minced)
- Half tablespoon of cumin

- Salt and pepper as per your taste
- Two tablespoons of paste of tomato
- Two cans of pinto beans (washed and rinsed)
- One cup of corn
- Five scallions (sliced)
- Eight tortillas
- 2 cups of cheese (shredded)
- Salsa for topping

Instructions:

1. Firstly, cook rice and set it aside.
2. In a broad skillet, warm oil over moderate flame. Add all spices, onion, garlic and tomatoes in it.
3. Cook, stirring regularly, for 12 minutes or until it turns golden.
4. Include the beans and one cup of water. Put a lid over the pan and boil it for 10 to 12 minutes or until thickened.
5. After this, add scallions and corn in it and let t cook for 5 minutes.
6. Prepare tortillas and fill it with bean mixture and cheese.
7. Assemble all the prepare ingredient together and place it in the baking dish and let it bake until the tortillas turn brown.
8. Serve it with salsa or any other topping.

❖ **Zucchini Enchiladas**

Period Required: 30 minutes

Servings: 5

Ingredients:
- Olive oil
- One onion (chopped)
- Two tablespoons of garlic (minced)
- One teaspoon of cumin
- Salt, pepper and chili as per your taste
- 1 cup of sauce enchilada
- Four zucchini (halved)
- 2 cups of cheddar cheese (shredded)

Instructions:
1. Firstly, preheat the oven to 250C. Warm the oil in a wide pan over moderate flame.
2. Add the onion, cumin, spices and garlic in it and let it simmer for 5-10 minutes or until it turns tender.
3. Insert 1 cup of enchilada sauce and let it cook for a while.
4. Peel thin slices of zucchini. Cover with a spoonful of cooked mixture and set out three slices, somewhat intertwined.
5. Wrap up and move to a tray for baking. Repeat with the mixture of remaining zucchini and prepared mixture.
6. Put the cheese over it.
7. Bake for 20 minutes, before the cheese, is melted and the enchiladas are cooked.
8. Serve it with sour cream or any other topping of your liking.

❖ **Mushroom and Onion Tacos**

Servings: 4

Period Required: 30 minutes

Ingredients:

- One tablespoon oil
- One onion (sliced)
- Three mushrooms (chopped properly)
- Two teaspoons taco seasoning
- Water
- Tortillas
- Half cup of fresco cheese (shredded)

Instruction:

1. Melt butter over mid to low flame in a pan. Cook the onion and mushrooms in it and let it cook for 7 minutes or until it turns soft.

2. Lower the heat and add seasonings, water and spices in it. Cook for about 5 minutes or before it consumes water.
3. Fill tortillas with the cooked mixture and put cheese over it.
4. Serve it.

- ❖ **Veggie Pizzadillas**

Servings: 4

Period Required: 30 minutes

Ingredients:
- Eight tortillas
- 1 cup of tomato pasta sauce
- 1 cup of mozzarella (shredded)
- Dried oregano
- Salt and pepper as per your taste
- Sliced vegetables of your liking
- Olive oil

Instructions:
1. Combine the sauce, cheese and spices in a bowl and mix it thoroughly.
2. Place over each tortilla, then put sliced vegetables over it.
3. Put oil and oregano in a pan and let it get warm for 3 minutes. Rub it over the pizza Dallas on either side.
4. Fry them on either side until they are golden and crisp.
5. Cut into wedges and serve in slices.

❖ **Mexican Meatless Lasagna**

Servings: 5

Period Taken: Fifty Minutes

Ingredients:
- 1 cup of corns
- Onion, tomatoes and chilies (chopped)
- Half cup of black beans (rinsed)
- Six tortillas
- 2 tablespoons of taco seasoning
- 1 cup red and green bell pepper (sliced)
- 1 cup of beans (refried)
- 1 cup sauce of enchilada

- 1 cup of cheddar cheese (shredded)

Instructions:

1. Firstly, preheat the oven to 350°C. Grease a baking dish and put it aside.
2. Mix the corn, tomatoes and chiles in a moderate dish. Place a broad pan over moderate flame.
3. Add wedges of tortillas, taco seasoning and soy sauce in it and let it cook for 4 minutes. Put it aside. Add remaining vegetable spices in a pan and let it cook for 10 minutes or until it turns tender.
4. In the baking tray, assemble all ingredients together and put cheese over it. You have to assemble it in layers.
5. Bake for about 20 minutes or until it turns brown.

❖ **Bean Pie**

Servings: 5

Time required: 60 minutes

Ingredients:

- Piecrusts
- Two eggs
- 1 cup of beans
- Evaporated milk
- Half cup of sugar
- Half tablespoon of spice pumpkin pie
- Salt as per your taste

- Cream whipped for topping

Instructions:

1. Firstly, preheat the oven to 270C. Place the piecrust into a baking pie dish.
2. In a cup, whisk together all other ingredients. Pour in the piecrust mixture.
3. Bake it for 50 minutes in a preheated oven. Let it cool for a while.
4. Top it with whipped cream and serve it.

❖ **Vegan Tacos**

Servings: 2

Time required: 20 minutes

Ingredients:

- 2 cups of beans
- 1 cup of tomato sauce
- 1 tablespoon of cumin
- One avocado (diced)
- Half cup of corn
- Eight shells of taco

Instructions:
1. Put a broad pan over moderate flame and cook beans, tomatoes and spices in it for 10 minutes.
2. Insert the bean mixture in the tacos and top it with toppings of your liking. Serve it with garnishing.

❖ **Red Beans and Rice Burritos**

Servings: 6

Time required: 35 minutes

Ingredients:
- Water
- 1 cup of brown rice
- 1 Onion and green pepper (chopped)
- Olive oil
- 1 teaspoon of garlic (minced)
- Salt and chili as per your taste
- One can of black beans (rinsed)

- Eight tortillas
- Salsa

Instructions:

1. Put a pan filled with water, rice and salt over moderate heat. Let it boil for a while until it is cooked.
2. Add oil, all other spices, onions, garlic and beans in another pan and let it cook for 10 minutes or until the mixture turn soft.
3. Add boiled rice in it and let it simmer for 4 minutes.
4. Fill each tortilla with the above prepared and put cheese and salsa over it.
5. Serve it.

❖ Chard Tacos

Time required: 20 minutes

Servings: 3

Ingredients:
- Olive oil
- One big onion (chopped)
- 2 teaspoons of garlic (minced)
- Water
- One bunch of Swiss chard (chopped)
- Salt and pepper as per your taste
- 8 tortillas
- 1 cup of fresco cheese (shredded)
- Salsa

Instructions:
1. Put a pan over a medium flame. Add oil, onions, garlic and all other spices in it. Let it cook until onion turns soft.
2. Add other ingredients in it. Put a lid over the pan. Simmer it for 8 minutes.
3. Set it aside.
4. Heat the tortillas in another heated pan on either side for roughly 1 minute. Cover the chard with the cooked tortillas and finish with the salsa or cheese.

❖ **Fried Avocado Tacos**

Time required: 20 minutes
Servings: 7

Ingredients:
- Half cup of wheat
- 2 Eggs
- 1 cup of breadcrumbs
- Two avocados (sliced)
- Oil
- Salt and pepper as per your taste
- 2 cups of cabbage (chopped)

- 1 cup of cheese (shredded)
- Salsa
- 8 Tortillas

Instructions:

1. In three different cups, put the rice, eggs, and breadcrumbs separately. Submerge the rims of the avocado in rice.
2. Cover with egg, then breadcrumbs.
3. In deep pan, heat oil over moderate flame. Fry the avocado, around 1 to 2 minutes per foot, until golden brown.
4. Segregate the avocado slices equally between the tortillas to build the tacos. Add cabbage, cheese and other seasonings on the top of it.

❖ **Vegan Mexican Rice**

Servings: 5

Period Required: 40 minutes

Ingredients:

- 2 cups of rice
- 1 cup of black beans
- Half cup of sweet corn
- One onion (chopped)
- One red bell pepper (sliced)
- Half teaspoon of sliced jalapeno
- Half teaspoon of garlic powder
- One cube of bouillon

- One tablespoon of tomato puree
- Lime zest
- Oil
- Water
- Salt as per you taste

Instructions:

1. Add oil, onion, spices, bell pepper, garlic, tomato paste and a cube of bouillon in a pan and put it over moderate flame. Let it cook for 5-10 minutes.
2. Then, add beans in it and let it cook until it is cooked. Add rice, water, spices in it and put a lid over it. Let it boil until the water is absorbed.
3. Squeeze the juice with fresh lime and serve it.

❖ Vegan Chickpea and Vegetable Tacos

Servings: 4

Time required: 15 minutes.

Ingredients:

- 2 cans of chickpeas (rinsed)
- Half cup of water
- 1 tablespoon of taco seasoning
- Eight shells of taco

Instructions:

1. Add the chickpeas, taco spices and water over a moderate flame in a skillet. Cook and mix for 5 to 7 minutes until fully cooked.
2. Mash the mixture of chickpeas to crush.
3. Divide the chickpea filling between the taco shells equally.

❖ Vegetarian Portabella Mushroom Enchilada

Servings: 5

Time took: 90 minutes

Ingredients:

- One tablespoon of vinegar

- One teaspoon of sugar
- Five tablespoons of fresh lime juice
- One big onion (chopped)
- One chipotle Chile
- Two tablespoon of heavy cream
- Salt and pepper as per your taste
- Vegetable oil
- Three big mushrooms (chopped)
- One clove of garlic (minced)
- 12 tortillas
- 6 ounces of fresh cheese (shredded)
- 1 cup of cheddar (shredded)

Instructions:

1. Firstly, preheat the oven to 250C.
2. Mix sugar, lime zest and syrup in a separate bowl.
3. Add Chile, half cup of milk, salt and cream in a blender. Blend it well. Set it aside.
4. Put pan with oil over moderate flame.
5. Add mushrooms, Chile, garlic, and onion in it. Fry them until mushrooms turn tender. Season it with spices.
6. In the meantime, heat tortillas in the microwave.
7. Grease baking dish with oil. Spread the cream sauce evenly in the baking dish.
8. Cover tortillas with cream sauce thoroughly. Put it in the baking dish.
9. Assemble all other ingredients over the tortillas.

10. Spoon the leftover sauce over the enchiladas, ensuring sure that the sauce is fully coated. Cover with cheddar.
11. Bake enchiladas for 35 minutes until the sides of the tortillas turn brown.
12. Serve it warm.

Chapter 03: Vegetarian Mexican Snacks Recipes

Whenever you are mild hungry and do not want to eat anything heavy, then snacks are the best option available to you. Snacks are also easy to make, and you can eat them at any-time. In this chapter, you will come to know about recipes of Vegetarian Mexican snacks that can be prepared easily by following given instructions.

❖ **Quick Microwave Nachos**

Serving: 1

Total time: 15 minutes

Ingredients:
- Tortilla chips (1 cup)
- Taco sauce (¼ cup)

- Mexican shredded cheese (1 cup)

Instructions:
1. Assemble the tortilla chips in any plate that is microwaveable.
2. Cover with tacos spices and cheese in a uniform way.
3. Let it microwave for 3 minutes uncovered. Put a cover on it and let it heat for one more minute or until cheese is completely melted.
4. Garnish it with preferred toppings and serve.

❖ **Cheese and Bell Pepper Quesadillas**

Servings: 20

Period Taken: Fifty minutes

Ingredients:
- One green bell pepper (washed and sliced)
- One red bell pepper (sliced)
- One yellow bell pepper (sliced)
- One onion (finely chopped)
- One tablespoon of garlic powder
- Pepper, chilies and salt as per your taste
- Butter
- ¼ tablespoon of cumin
- 1 cup of cream cheese (whisked)
- ½ cup of cheddar cheese (shredded)
- Tortillas

- Sour cream and salsa for topping

Instructions:

1. Put a pan with butter over moderate flame and let the butter melts.
2. Add bell peppers, garlic powder, chopped onions and cumin in it.
3. Let it cook for 3-4 minutes and then add spices in it. Let it simmer for 2 minutes.
4. Drain extra oil from the mixture and set it aside.
5. Mix the chilies, cream cheese and one teaspoon of fresh garlic together in a separate bowl. Then, add the cheddar cheese and mix it thoroughly.
6. Spread each tortilla with between 4 teaspoons of the cheese mixture.
7. Top it with cooked mixture and then roll tortillas. Put the butter over the tortilla thinly and dust it with cumin or any other spices. Put the tortilla slices on a thinly greased baking dish.
8. Heat the oven at 400 degrees.
9. Bake for around 15 minutes or until tortillas turns brown.
10. Cut tortillas into slices. Garnish it with salsa or any other topping of your liking and serve.

❖ Nachos with Vegan Cheese Sauce

Servings: 3

Time took: 30 minutes

Ingredients:
- Cashew casserole (1 cup)
- Olive oil
- Half of the onion (finely chopped)
- Two cloves of garlic (minced)
- Chilies, pepper and salt as per your taste
- Half cup of milk
- One tablespoon of yeast
- One tablespoon of lime zest
- Mustard (optional)
- Water

- Tortilla chips
- 1 cup of black beans (rinsed and drained)
- Salsa
- Guacamole

Instructions:
1. Put the cashews in a shallow pan and water in it at room temperature. Let it simmer for minimum one hour to two hours. Then, drain water from it.
2. Over moderate flame, heat the oil in a pan. Add the oil, accompanied by the onion. Let it cook for a few minutes and continue stirring it.
3. Add the garlic and all spices in it. Stir and let it cook for 4-5 minutes. After cooking, set it aside.
4. To a mixer, put soaked cashews, a mixture of onion, milk, yeast, lime zest, mustard, salt and pepper as per your taste. Put a lid on it and blend it well. Add ¼ cup of water in it to gain uniform consistency.
5. In a saucepan, put the blended sauce and cook over a moderate flame, stir continuously. It should not be thickened.
6. Start piling up half of the chips on plates, put the cooked sauce over it, and sprinkle with cheese sauce and salsa.
7. Garnish it with guacamole. Serve it.

❖ Mango Salsa

Servings: 5

Time took: 10 minutes

Ingredients:
- One mango (peeled and sliced)
- Half cup of cucumber
- One teaspoon jalapeno
- ½ cup onion (finely sliced)
- Lime zest
- Coriander leaves
- Pepper and salt as per your taste

Instructions:
1. Mix all the ingredients, spices and lime juice together and blend it properly with the help of a blender.
2. Taste it, if you want to add more salt and pepper, you can add it. Serve it.

❖ **Bread Rolls**

Servings: 16

Time took: 3 hours

Ingredients:
- 2 cups of warm water
- Two teaspoons of yeast
- One tablespoon of sugar
- Vegetable oil
- Salt and pepper as per your taste
- 4 cups of flour

Instructions:
1. Place a wide bowl. Mix the water, sugar, and yeast together in it.
2. Set it aside for around 12 minutes or until it turns creamy. Put the oil, salt, and flour to the above mixture.
3. Mix the mixture together and slowly add more flour to it as per your need and knead the mixture to form a dough.
4. Roll out on a gentle sheet pan and knead for around 5 minutes until it is smooth and flexible. Position the dough in the tub and gently sprinkle oil over it and cover it with a lid.
5. Set it aside for 1 hour and let it rise until it turns twice in size.
6. Dampen the dough, then on a floured board, turn it out. Cut the dough into 16 equal parts and mould into balls that are circular. Place them apart on thinly lubricated baking sheets. Top the rolls with a moist cloth and let them put aside for around 40 minutes before they have risen in size.
7. In the meanwhile, preheat the oven up to 200C.
8. Put a baking dish in an oven.
9. Let it bake for 25 minutes or until it turns golden brown.

❖ **Huevos Diablos**

Period Required: 40 minutes

Servings: 6

Ingredients:
- Olive oil
- One onion (chopped)
- One tablespoon of garlic
- 1 cup of tomatoes (chopped)
- One teaspoon of sauce from Worcestershire
- ¾ cup of Parmesan cheese (shredded)
- Six eggs
- Butter
- Six tortillas (corn)

Instructions:
1. Warm olive oil over a moderate flame in a large frying pan. Fry, the onion for around 6 minutes or until it, turns smooth, transparent, and brown. Stir in the garlic and let it simmer for 1 minute.
2. Stir in the spices, tomato sauce and other sauce.
3. Carry it to a simmer at low flame and cook for around 10 minutes.
4. In the meanwhile, the oven should be preheated 175C.
5. Put a bowl and mix in tomato sauce with shredded Parmesan cheese.
6. In 6 tiny oven-safe cups that greased with oil, put a mixture of sauce in it. On top of each one, split one egg and sprinkle with butter. Toss with the Parmesan cheese.

7. Bake it for 25 minutes in the oven, uncovered, or until the egg whites are firm, but the yolks are still fluffy.
8. Serve it with tortillas or bread.

- ❖ **Grilled Pepper Popper**

Servings: 6

Time took: 35 minutes

Ingredients:
- ¼ cup of cream (whisked)
- 16 sweet peppers
- 1 cup of Mexican cheese (shredded)
- One tomato (finely chopped)
- ½ cup of onion (finely chopped)
- Two tablespoons of cilantro
- Salt and pepper as per your taste

Instructions:
1. Put a spoon of sour cream into a bag in the freezer and let it cool for a while.
2. In the meanwhile, preheat the grill to a moderate temperature.
3. Rinse or wash the peppers and cut it into lengthwise in halves. You also have to remove their seeds.
4. Blend the cheese, onions, cabbage, cilantro and spices together in a shallow dish.

5. Fill the pepper halves equally with the mixture of cheese and press it so that it can fill it with leaving any hollows.
6. Put it into a baking dish and let it bake from the above side.
7. Cook until the hems are scorched and mildly burnt for around 5 minutes.
8. Shift the peppers to the plate with the help of a large spatula.
9. Cut off the sour cream in the bag and pour over the hot peppers equally.
10. Immediately serve.

❖ **Fried Jalapenos**

Servings: 6

Time took: 20 minutes

Ingredients:
- Flour (1 cup)
- Salt, chilies and pepper as per your taste
- Two eggs
- Oil
- 2 cups of jalapeno peppers (chopped)

Instructions:
1. In a cup, blend together the flour, salt, spices, garlic powder, and eggs.

2. Add the oil in a deep fryer and let it heat to 180C.
3. In the above-mixed batter, insert the cut jalapenos. Place the deep fryer with the battered jalapenos.
4. When they rise to the top of the liquid, the jalapenos are completely fried. They are meant to be lightly browned and crispy.

❖ Grilled Corn

Time took: 50 minutes

Servings: 6

Ingredients:
- Eight ears of corn
- Salt and pepper as per your taste

For BBQ butter:
- One tablespoon of canola oil
- Half red onion (chopped)
- One tablespoon of garlic powder
- One tablespoon of paprika
- One teaspoon of cumin seeds (roasted)
- Chilies, salt and pepper as per your taste
- Half cup of water
- Butter

Instructions:
1. Firstly, heat the grill up to medium temperature or flame.
2. Take the outer hollows of corns to the neck. Completely remove it by hand from each ear of grain.
3. Cover the husks back in order and place the maize ears for 15 minutes in a wide bowl of cold water with salt.

4. Drain the water from maize and let it dry for a while. Set up the corn on the grill, close the cover of the grill and let it cook for 15 minutes, rotating every 5 minutes or until its corn turn tender.
5. Using the BBQ butter, spread over the corn when served.
6. Preheat over a moderate flame in a wide pan. Insert the onion and cook for 2 or 3 minutes until it is tender. Add all other ingredients in it and let it cook for a while. Add water and spices in it and let it boil for 5 minutes or until the mixture thickens. Set it aside and let it cool for a while.
7. In a food processor, put the butter and above mixture in it. Grind it well until a uniform consistency is created.
8. Put it aside for 30 minutes before using it further.

❖ **Spicy Refried Beans**

Servings: 2

The period required: 35 minutes

Ingredients:
- One onion (chopped)
- One pepper jalapeno (chopped)
- One tablespoon of garlic powder
- Oil
- 1 cup of beans (refried)

- Water
- Pepper and salt as per your taste
- ½ teaspoon of cumin field

Instructions:

1. Put a medium-size deep-pan above a medium flame.
2. Place beans and shredded Monterey Jack cheese in it. Add water in it that should be around 2 inches.
3. Carry the beans to a simmer. After some time, remove it from the flame and set it aside.
4. Meanwhile, the chiles are washed and dried. Cover them with oil and put on a plain baking pan under the oven for around 10 minutes, rotating once in a while. When the skin turns blackish and blistered, remove it from the oven.
5. Chop the garlic and chiles. Set them aside
6. Remove the beans mixture from the bowl after 1 hour, and put them in the slow cooker. To be around 1 inch above the beans, cover with adequate water. Include the diced chiles, ginger, onions and ground garlic.
7. Cook for 8 hours on high temperature.
8. You can spice them and consume them as they are and you can refry them when the beans are cooked.

❖ **Chipotle Lime Corn Cobs**

Servings: 6

Time took: 40 minutes

Ingredients:
- Six ears of sweet corn
- Mayonnaise
- One chipotle pepper sauce
- One tablespoon of coriander
- One tablespoon of lime zest
- ½ cup of Asiago cheese (shredded)

Instructions:
1. Start peeling the corn husks gently.
2. Maize is rewrapped in husks and tied with kitchen cord. In a large pan, put the cold water along with salt. Let it soak for 30 minutes.
3. Grill the corn, and cover for 25 minutes or until it turns tender after turning sometimes.
4. Place the remaining ingredients in a shallow dish. Mix them thoroughly. Over each sweet corn, add one tablespoon of this mixture on top.
5. Sprinkle with cheese and some lime zest. Just serve it.

❖ **Creamy Pumpkin Soup**

Servings: 5

Time took: 50 minutes

Ingredients:
- Two tablespoons of butter

- Two teaspoons of sugar
- Four bread slices

For the soup:
- 1 cup onion (chopped)
- Sugar
- 2 cups of water
- Pumpkin puree
- Salt and pepper as per your taste
- ¼ tablespoon of ginger powder
- 1 cup of milk (whipped)

Instructions:
1. Firstly, preheat the oven to 200 degrees C.
2. Mix the melted butter, sugar and cinnamon to produce coleslaw.
3. Range the butter mixture equally over one side of each piece of bread. Put bread on a greased baking dish, buttered side up.
4. Bake it for 5 minutes or just until the bread is crisp. Start cutting each bread slice into eight little triangles.
5. Simmer the onion in a medium saucepan with butter until it turns soft.
6. Add water in it. Put a lid over it and reduce the flame to low and simmer for 15 minutes. Bring it to a boil.
7. Move the above mixture into the blender. Blend it until it turns smooth.
8. Shift the mixture back to the skillet.

9. Add the water, pumpkin, salt, ground cinnamon, ground ginger and ground pepper to the pan. Mix it well. Carry it to a boil. Put a lid over it and reduce the flame. Let it simmer, stirring periodically, for ten more minutes.
10. Stir in the cream and heat up. Serve it.

❖ **Grilled Guacamole**

Servings: 4

Time took: 20 minutes

Ingredients:
- Olive Oil
- Four avocados (peeled)
- Lime zest (1 tablespoon)
- Salt and pepper as per your taste
- ¼ onion (finely chopped)

Instructions:
1. Initially, preheat barbecue grill on low flame. Grease it well.
2. Peel and cut an avocado in halves. Grease half of each avocado gently with oil.
3. Set the cut-side avocados down on the barbecue. Cover and cook, around 5 minutes per hand, until warmed through and grill marks emerge.

4. To a wide cup, move the avocados and let them cool slightly. With a fork, break. Sprinkle in the lime zest and the spices to the seasoning.
5. Serve with chips instantly.

❖ **Mexican Bread Tartlets**

Servings: 6

Time took: 35 minutes

Ingredients:
- Six bread slices
- 1 cup of cheese (shredded)

- One potato (baked and sliced)
- One onion (chopped)
- One tomato (finely chopped)
- Six olives (pitted)
- Salt, pepper and chili as per your taste
- Half teaspoon of basil and oregano powder
- Olive oil

Instructions:

1. Trim the sides of bread slices. Then, place these slices in greased muffin tins.
2. Sprinkle some oil over it.
3. Bake at 200C for 10-12 minutes in a preheated oven until the bread is crisp and browned.
4. Meanwhile, chop all the vegetables.
5. Remove the tray from oven and place the apples, tomatoes and onions in it.
6. Also, sprinkle all spices and shredded cheese over it.
7. Bake in the oven for 10 minutes or until cheese gets brown.
8. Serve any garnishing of your liking.

❖ **Mexican French Fries**

Servings: 2

Period Required: 30 minutes

Ingredients:

- Sour cream
- Fries
- Mexican cheese dip
- Onion (chopped)
- Taco seasoning

Instructions:
1. Firstly, preheat the deep fryer. Fry fries in it for 15 minutes or until it turns golden brown.
2. Assemble fries and all other ingredients in a plate and heat it in a microwave for 3 minutes or until cheese melts.

❖ **Crispy Fried Cauliflower**

Servings: 4

Time took: 35 minutes

Ingredients:
- One cauliflower (washed and chopped)
- Salt and pepper as per your taste
- One teaspoon of onion powder, oregano, paprika, and garlic powder
- Flour (2 cups)
- Two tablespoons of cornstarch
- One cup of soy milk
- One tablespoon of cider vinegar
- Oil

Instructions:
1. Combine all spices in a shallow cup. Mix thoroughly.
2. Add half of the spice, corn starch, apple cider, soy milk and flour in a separate bowl and mix it thoroughly.
3. Over the cauliflower, pour the above mixture and combine well until they are covered.
4. Let it cool for 1 hour in a fridge.
5. Put a deep fry pan with oil over a moderate heat and let it for a while. Put pieces of cauliflower in oil and let it fry until it turns brown.
6. Serve with any sauce and garnishing of your liking.

❖ **Mexican Stuffed Cheese Potatoes**

Servings: 4

The period required: 35 minutes

Ingredients:

- Four potatoes
- 1 cup of black bean (rinsed)
- Vegetables of your liking (chopped)
- 1 cup of cheese (shredded)
- One tomato (chopped)
- Sour cream as garnishing (optional)

Instructions:

1. Put washed and peeled potatoes in the oven for 10 minutes and let it bake.
2. In meanwhile, chopped all vegetables and let it cook over moderate heat in a pan along with spices.
3. By using a knife, cut a shape of X on each baked potato. Use a fork or spoon to make a void in it.
4. Fill out that void with cooked mixture and sprinkle cheese over it. Let it heat for 4 minutes in an oven or until cheese is melted.
5. Garnish it with sour cream and serve.

❖ **Tomato Cheese Toast**

Servings: 2

Time took: 30 minutes

Ingredients:

- Four bread slices

- Four small pieces of cheese
- One tomato (finely chopped)
- Spices
- Olive Oil

Instructions:

1. Firstly, preheat the furnace to 200°C.
2. Grease the baking sheet well with oil.
3. Place bread slices in it and put over the cheese and other ingredients over it.
4. Bake until it mixes with the cheese.

❖ **Guacamole Onion Rings**

Servings: 6

Time took: 60 minutes

Ingredients:
- Three avocados (peeled and sliced)
- Lime zest
- One onion (finely sliced)
- Cilantro
- Garlic
- Salt and pepper as per your taste
- Flour for coating
- Two eggs (well beaten)
- 2 cups of panko bread crumbs
- Oil for frying

Instructions:
1. Mash the boiled avocados with lime juice in a mixing cup.
2. Combine all chopped vegetables and spices in a separate bowl.
3. Break the onion into chunks. Separate the layers cautiously into separate circles—lay-out onion rings on a tray.
4. Mix avocado mixture with each chunk of onion. Set it aside in the fridge.
5. In three distinct bowls, incorporate the flour, beating eggs, and panko breadcrumbs.
6. First, roll each one in flour, then eggs, then breadcrumbs. Coat the egg again and brush the breadcrumbs for the final time.

7. Place a pan with oil over moderate heat and fry those chunks with coating in it until it turns brown.
8. Sprinkle with lime juice and salt. Use sour cream to serve.

❖ **Crusty Potato Fingers**

Servings: 4

Time took: 40 minutes

Ingredients:
- 2 cups of boiled potatoes
- Half cup of semolina
- Salt, pepper and chilies as per your taste
- Coriander
- Warm water
- Oil for frying

Instructions:
1. Put half a cup of water and semolina together in a cup. Mix it well and set it aside.
2. Mix semolina mixture and boiled potatoes together.
3. Now, add all spices in it.
4. Mix it thoroughly and set it aside in a fridge.
5. Fry these in any shape of your liking in a frying pan over moderate flame for 4 minutes or until they turn brown.

6. In the above manner, cook all the potato fingers.
7. Serve with any sauce of your liking.

❖ **Grilled Salsa Roja**

Portions: 3 cups

Period Required: 30 minutes

Ingredients:
- Eight cherry tomatoes
- Half onion
- Four chiles
- Three cloves of garlic (minced)
- Salt, pepper and chilies as per your taste

Instructions:
1. Firstly, preheat the greased grill with medium flame.
2. Grill all vegetables over a preheated grill for about 5-8 minutes or until they are completely cooked.
3. Set them aside to cool down a bit.
4. In a blender, make a purée of the grilled vegetables and spices.
5. Serve with anything of your liking.

Chapter 04: Vegetarian Mexican Dinner Recipes

Dinner recipes are similar to lunch recipes because both are quite heavy. People usually either eat lunch heavy or dinner heavy. In this chapter, you will come to know about Vegetarian Mexican Dinner recipes. They are very lavish and full of flavors. Following are some amazing Mexican dinner recipes that you can make at home:

❖ **Mexican Sheet Pan Supper**

Servings: 3

Total time: 30 minutes

Ingredients:
- One sweet potato

- Two bell peppers (washed and sliced)
- One onion (finely sliced)
- One corn (drained)
- 1 cup of black beans (soaked and drained)
- Oil
- Spices
- For the topping: salsa

Instructions:

1. Cut sweet potatoes into cubes and let it boil in a pan filled with water for 13 minutes or until it turns tender.
2. You should preheat the oven up to 200C.
3. Grease a baking dish and put all ingredients and boiled sweet potatoes in it.
4. Let it bake for 20 minutes.
5. Serve it with a topping of salsa.

❖ **Taco Soup**

Servings: 7

Total time: 25 minutes

Ingredients:

- Oil
- ½ onion (finely sliced)
- Two cloves of garlic (minced properly)
- Salt, pepper, paprika, cumin and chilies as per your taste

- 1 cup of tomato (chopped or puree)
- 1 ½ cups of black beans (rinsed and soaked)
- One green chili (sliced)
- 2 cups of broth of vegetables
- 1 cup of corn
- 1 cup of cheese (shredded)

Instructions:

1. Put a pan with oil over moderate flame and let it heat for 2 minutes.
2. Add onions, garlic, spices and tomatoes. Let it cook for 10 minutes or until onions become translucent.
3. Add broth in it and put a lid over a pan and let it simmer for 15 minutes or until broth thickens.
4. For taste, add lime zest at the end.
5. Serve with garnishing of cheese.

❖ **Roasted Cauliflower Street Tacos**

Servings: 5

Time took: 40 minutes

Ingredients:

- 2 cups of cabbage (finely chopped)
- One tablespoon of apple cider vinegar
- One teaspoon of lime zest
- ½ tablespoon of honey (only for vegans)
- Salt and pepper as per your taste

- 2 cups of cauliflower (finely chopped)
- 1 cup of chickpeas (soaked and drained)
- Olive oil
- Salt, pepper, cumin and chili as per your taste
- Tortillas

For the sauce:
- One avocado
- One garlic (minced)
- Olive oil
- Lime zest
- Parsley
- Salt and pepper

Instructions:
1. Firstly, preheat the oven up to 200C.
2. Make slaw by mixing the ingredients above mentioned.
3. Then, make a sauce by blending all ingredients mentioned above.
4. Combine all the ingredients for Cauliflower Filling in a bowl. Place on a greased baking dish.
5. Let it bake for 25 minutes or until it turns brown.
6. Assemble all baked and mixed products over tortillas and serve.

❖ **Soyrizo Potato Tacos**

Servings: 10

Time took: 40 minutes

Ingredients:
- Two yellow potatoes (chopped)
- Olive oil
- Salt, pepper, chili, oregano and cumin as per your taste
- Ten ounces of soyrizo
- Ten tortillas
- Chopped lettuce for serving

Instructions:
1. In a broad bowl, place the cut potatoes and all spices in it. Mix it thoroughly.

2. Meanwhile, preheat the oven up to 220C.
3. Bake coated potatoes in the oven for 25 minutes or until it turns tender.
4. Then, you have to fry the potatoes for 4-5 minutes.
5. Prepare the soyrizo over a moderate flame in a pan for 5 minutes or until it is cooked perfectly.
6. Assemble potatoes first in each tortilla and put soyrizo mixture over it and then add your likeable topping over it.
7. Serve warm.

❖ Mexican Chili Rellenos

Servings: 6

Time took: 40 minutes

Ingredients:
- Six new chili peppers (sliced)
- 1 cup of Mexican cheese (strips)
- Chopped vegetables of your liking
- ½ tablespoon of baking powder
- 1 cup of flour
- The oil used for frying
- Eggs as per your requirement

Instructions:
1. Firstly, preheat the oven and place the oven rack in it.
2. Cover baking dish with foil and bake pepper in it for 10 minutes or until it turns blistered.

3. Let it set aside to cool. Peel the peppers under cold water and slice it to only get its long sides.
4. You have to sprinkle oil over it and fill it with cheese strips.
5. Lightly bake it to melt the cheese in it.
6. Meanwhile, whisk eggs and baking powder with the help of beater. Add flour in it.
7. Sauté the chopped vegetables in the pan over medium flame until the vegetables turn tender. Set it aside.
8. Put these vegetables in the pepper.
9. Cover all sides of pepper with a flour-egg mixture and fry it in frying pan until it turns brown and crisp.
10. Repeat this process for all peppers.
11. Serve it with your favorite sauce.

❖ Lentil Tacos

Servings: 2

Time took: 40 minutes

Ingredients:
- Olive oil
- One onion (finely sliced)
- Two teaspoons of garlic powder
- One cup of lentils (dried)
- One cup of vegetables (chopped)
- Salt, chili, paprika and pepper as per your taste
- Half cup of salsa (can be used as a topping)

Instructions:
1. Place a pan with two tablespoons of oil over a moderate flame and heat it for 3 minutes.
2. Place sliced onions in it and let it simmer for about 5 minutes or until onions begin to tender.
3. Add garlic, vegetable stock, spices and all other ingredients in it and let it cook for 30 minutes or until it turns tender.
4. When it is cooked, serve it with your favorite topping.

❖ Mashed Potato and Mashed Vegetable Enchilada

Serving: 5-6

Time took: 90 minutes

Ingredients:
- One broccoli (chopped into florets)
- 7 ounces of mushrooms
- 2 ½ zucchini (chopped)
- 1 ½ cups of carrots (chopped)
- Olive oil
- Salt and pepper as per your taste
- Water (2 or 3 cups)
- Milk (1 cup)
- Butter (half cup)
- Potato flakes (instant packet)
- 6 Tortillas
- 2 cups of enchilada sauce
- 2 cups of cheese (shredded)

Instructions:
1. Firstly, preheat the oven up to 200C.
2. Chop all vegetables as per instructions. Put them in greased baking dish. Sprinkle spices and oil over it. Bake for 30 minutes in an oven or until vegetables turns tender.
3. Add mashed potato flakes, milk, butter and water in a pot. Put a lid over the pot. Let it boil until it is cooked.
4. Sprinkle oil over tortillas. Reheat tortillas in a non-stick pan over moderate heat.
5. Assemble all cooked products in the middle of each tortilla. Spread sauce, spices and cheese over it. Roll it as you pleased.

6. Place tortillas in a baking dish and spread the remaining sauce and cheese over all tortillas evenly.
7. Bake it for 5-10 minutes or until cheese is properly melted.
8. Serve it.

❖ **Sweet Potato Nachos**

Servings: 6

Time took: 45 minutes

Ingredients:
- Three sweet potatoes (slice into circular shapes)
- Olive oil
- Salt, chili and pepper as per your taste
- ½ tablespoon of garlic powder
- ½ tablespoon of paprika powder
- ½ cup of black beans (soaked, rinsed and drained)
- ½ cup of cheese (shredded)
- ½ cup of tomatoes (chopped)
- Half cup of avocado (chopped)

Instructions:
1. Firstly, preheat the furnace up to 220C.
2. Place a foil over baking dish and grease it with oil.
3. Place sliced sweet potatoes in a baking dish. Sprinkle spices over it and let it bake for 10 minutes. Make sure to rotate the sides of sweet potato.

4. Add beans and cheese in the above baking dish. Let it bake for another 10 minutes or until beans turn soft.
5. Serve it with any sauce.

❖ **Tofu Tacos with Chili**

Servings: 7

Time took: 60 minutes

Ingredients:

- 16 ounces of tofu (pressed and dried)
- ¼ cup of soy sauce
- One tablespoon of lemon zest
- Vegan mayonnaise
- Salt, pepper and chilies as per your taste
- 1 cup of cabbage and avocado (chopped)
- Seven tortillas
- Half cup of scallions

Instructions:

1. Cut tofu into 1-inch cubes.
2. Sprinkle lime zest and soy sauce over the tofu and place it aside.
3. Fry the chopped vegetables in a pan over moderate flame.
4. Meanwhile, coat tofu with corn starch and mix it in the above pan. Cook it until it turns brown, and vegetables turn tender.
5. Reheat the tortillas on the skillet.

6. Assemble the cooked mixture along with sauce over the tortillas.
7. Serve it with any topping.

❖ Jalapeno Chickpea Mac and Cheese Pasta

Servings: 8

Time took: 45 minutes

Ingredients:
- 17 ounces of chickpea and lentil pasta
- 2 ½ jalapenos (chopped without seeds)
- 1 cup of chickpea (rinsed and drained)
- Salt, paprika, chili, cumin and pepper as per your taste
- Garlic powder
- Olive oil

- ¼ cup of milk
- ¼ cup of broth (vegetables)
- ½ tablespoon of yeast
- Two tablespoons of flour

Instructions:

1. Preheat the furnace up to 220C. Fill a big pot with 6 cups of water and put a lid over it and bring it to a boil.
2. Mix chickpeas with spices. Spread and bake on a baking sheet for 18 minutes or until it turns tender.
3. Boil pasta in the above boiling water as per given instruction behind the package. Drain it well.
4. Sprinkle spices over pasta and place it in a baking dish. Let it bake for 3 minutes.
5. Meanwhile, blend coconut milk, broth, yeast and flour in another deep saucepan. Let it cook until it thickened. When the sauce is prepared, let it put aside.
6. Mix the pasta, chickpea with the sauce.
7. Garnish and serve with cilantro.

❖ **Sofritas Tofu Burrito**

Servings: 8

Time took: 60 minutes

Ingredients:

- One block tofu (dried properly and cut into cubes)
- Olive oil

- One cup of each red and green pepper (diced)
- One cup of onion (diced)
- Salt, pepper, chili and cumin as per your taste
- One tablespoon of tomato puree
- 1 cup of tomatoes (roasted and chopped)
- Half cup of broth (vegetable)

Instructions:
1. Firstly, preheat the oven up to 220C. Grease a baking dish.
2. Place cubes of tofu in the baking dish and sprinkle oil over it. Bake it for 10 minutes or more. Then, set it aside.
3. For the preparation of sofritas, sauté all the vegetables and spices in a deep pan.
4. Add baked tofu, broth and spices (if you want to) in the above deep pan. Put a lid on it and boil it for 15 minutes over low flame.
5. Thicken the consistency of mixture as per your liking.
6. Add lime zest over it and serve in a dish.

❖ **Spinach Tortillas**

Servings: 6

Period Required: 25 minutes

Ingredients:
- Flour (2 cups)
- Cooked spinach (1 cup)

- Water
- Salt and pepper as per your taste

Instructions:
1. Firstly, cook spinach as per your liking.
2. Blend the cooked spinach, and you can also add spices in it as per your taste.
3. Knead dough by mixing spinach puree, water and salt.
4. Dust the flour on a board and cut the dough into around 6-8 pieces. Roll the portions into balls with your hands to use.
5. Make tortillas by using these dough balls.
6. Cook tortillas in a skillet over a high flame. You can also add oil to it.
7. Carefully cook tortilla from both sides.
8. Repeat the process.
9. Serve all tortillas with a sauce of your liking.

❖ **Mexican Pasta Salad**

Servings: 6

Period Required: 25 minutes

Ingredients:
- One packet of pasta
- 1 cup of corn (drained)
- One can of black beans (soaked and drained)
- Olive oil
- One onion and bell pepper (chopped)

- ½ tomato (sliced)
- Cilantro
- 1 cup of cheese (shredded)

Ingredients for Dressing:

- Olive oil
- Fresh juice of a lime
- Two tablespoons of garlic
- One teaspoon of honey
- Half teaspoon of cumin
- Half teaspoon of paprika
- Salt
- Pepper

Instructions:

1. Cook the pasta according to the box instructions.
2. Combine the cooled spaghetti, rice, beans, olives, bell pepper, tomatoes and red onion in a wide dish.
3. Mix above ingredients of dressing to prepare a dressing for this recipe.
4. Put it over the pasta mixture. Mix it thoroughly.
5. Toss cilantro on the top of it.
6. Cover with the cheese and serve it.

❖ **Tomatillo Poblano White Beans**

Servings: 6

Total time: 40 minutes

Ingredients:
- 2 cups Tomatillos diced
- 1 cup poblano (sliced)
- 1 cup of onion (chopped)
- One jalapeno (sliced and without seeds)
- Salt and pepper as per your taste
- ½ teaspoon of cumin
- 1 cup of dried and soaked beans
- 1 cup of water or more
- One tablespoon of oregano

Instructions:
1. Blend all vegetables together. Blend until the veggies are thin, but not purified.
2. Over the moderate fire, pour the blended veggies in a deep pan. Add spices in it and let it cook for a while.
3. Add the beans, water and oregano to the above mixture and swirl to mix it. Put on the cover and let it boil over low heat for 30 minutes.
4. Prior to serving, apply salt and pepper to taste.

❖ **Casserole and Cheese**

Cooking Time: 35 minutes
Serving: 9

Ingredients:

- Salt and pepper, to taste
- Sour cream, as required
- Onion, one
- Minced garlic, three
- Mixed cheese, one cup
- Avocado, one
- Jalapeno, one
- Taco seasoning, one teaspoon
- Tortillas, nine
- Tomatoes, one
- Mix vegetables, half cup
- Vegetable oil, two teaspoons
- Cilantro, as required

Instructions:

1. Add the vegetable oil and cook the onions in a pan.
2. Add the minced garlic and cook.
3. Cook well and add tomatoes, taco seasoning, salt, and pepper into the mixture.
4. Add the mix vegetables and cook for two minutes.
5. Transfer the mixture into a baking dish and top with cheese blend.
6. Bake it for five minutes.
7. Add the cilantro on top and serve it with tortillas and desired toppings.

❖ Spicy Vegan Tofu Enchilada

Servings: 5-6

Time took: 40 minutes

Ingredients:
- Six light taco shells or tortillas
- One pack of tofu (dried and cut into cubes)
- Olive oil
- Two teaspoons of seasoning of taco
- Diced tomatoes
- 1 cup of black beans (rinsed and soaked)
- One diced onion

Instructions:
1. Firstly, preheat the oven up to 220C.
2. Dry out tofu completely. Cut into cubes.
3. Sprinkle seasoning over tofu. Place it in a skillet with oil over moderate flame and cook until it turns brown.
4. Mix the peas, black beans and onion in a bowl and put aside meanwhile the tofu is frying.
5. Mix together the sauce and chipotle seasoning in a different bowl and set aside. Take half cup of the sauce and dump it into a greased baking dish to scatter the sauce out over the dish.

6. To prepare the enchiladas: dump into one tortilla a tablespoon of the tomato mixture, then place a tablespoon of the fried tofu. Fold the tortilla and bring the part of the fold down into the baking dish. Repeat this step until all the enchiladas are completed.
7. Add the remaining mixture sauce over the enchiladas and let it bake for 17 minutes.
8. Serve it.

- ❖ **Crockpot Quinoa Tacos**

Servings: 5

Time took: 30 minutes

Ingredients:
- 1 of a cup of quinoa
- ½ cup of vegetable broth
- 1 cup of beans
- One diced tomatoes
- Taco seasoning

Instructions:
1. In a stockpot, combine all ingredients together.
2. Add taco seasoning in it.
3. Cook for three hours, on high temperature.
4. Serve it with tortillas.

❖ Colorful Vegetable Fajitas

Servings: 4

Time took: 40 minutes

Ingredients:
- Eight tortillas of flour
- Vegetable oil
- One red onion
- One green bell pepper (chopped)
- One red bell pepper (chopped)
- One teaspoon of garlic (minced)
- Salsa
- Salt and pepper as per your taste
- ½ tablespoon of cilantro

Instructions:
1. Firstly, preheat oven at 220C. Grease baking dish.
2. Place the tortillas in the oven. Bake until fully cooked.
3. Heat oil over a moderate flame in a pan. Add all spices and ingredients in it except veggies. Let it cook for 5-10 minutes.
4. Stir in the veggies with the squash. Cover, then let it simmer for more five minutes.
5. Sprinkle with cheese and cilantro and spoon the vegetable mixture equally down the centers of the soft tortillas. Roll up some tortillas, then serve.

❖ Asparagus and Cheese Quesadillas

Serving: 5

Time taken: 35 minutes

Ingredients:

- Olive oil
- Half pound of asparagus (chopped)
- Salt and pepper
- 2 tortillas of flour
- 4 ounces of cheese
- ½ cup of new cilantro (chopped)

Instructions:

1. In a pan over moderate flame, heat olive oil and cook the asparagus, swirling periodically, until it turns soft. Turn off the heat and season with spices.
2. Spread cheese over one surface of each tortilla. On each tortilla, position the asparagus and cilantro and roll half the tortillas over the ingredients to create quesadillas.
3. Over moderate flame, put the quesadillas in a pan and cook for 5 minutes on each hand, or until it is lightly browned.
4. Garnish with according to your taste and choice.

Conclusion

Mexican cooking is incredibly vast and amazing. It started from Mexico yet got popular enough to spread worldwide, and it is being eaten everywhere on the planet. The individuals of the United States of America love Mexican food, and they devour it on a daily basis.

Mexicans food is basically related to carnivorous eating, but with the time, Mexicans are embracing vegetarian and vegan diets too. If you study more about Mexican cuisines then, you will find out that vegetarian Mexican cuisines are way lesser than non-vegetarian cuisines. Mexico is mostly about citrus fruits, varieties of legumes, a broad selection of spices, and a preference for new cooking ingredients. It is a meat-focused country, and vegetarianism is not popular, however, luckily, there are vegetarian ingredients in many dishes, such as corn tortillas, rice, cheese, and vegetables.

Enchilada, Quesadilla, Burritos, Meatless Lasagna, Pies, Vegan burgers, Tortillas and much more are the best options for vegetarians in Mexico. At street stalls, these fast and inexpensive snacks can be found. Most of these are based on corn tortillas, and you can typically get vegetarian versions and then liven them up with typical toppings such as salsas, even though it is only cheese. In this book, we have given 77 distinct recipes of Vegetarian Mexican cuisine that include assorted dishes that you would love.

The given recipes incorporate solid breakfast, lunch, snacks and dinner. Most importantly, these recipes are all vegetarian in nature. An individual who does not normally cook, for the most part, can undoubtedly make every one of these recipes with the definite fixing rundown and simple to adhere directions that are referenced with every recipe in the book. After reading this book, you will be able to make delicious Vegetarian Mexican recipes at home.

Made in the USA
Coppell, TX
22 August 2021